SELAH'S
Painted Dream

*Thirteen-year-old Selah's equestrian aspirations are
trampled when moving away threatens to rip her from
her beloved horse. Selah sits deep in the saddle, presses
her heels down, and gallops after her dream.*

Dedication

Thanks to my amazing SCBWI critique group, *Charles Trevino*, *Mary Riser*, and the cast of critters.

Thanks to my husband, *David*, daughter, *Sarah*, and son, *Christopher*, for the constant encouragement.

Thanks to the talented *Elena Shved* for the perfect portrait of this horse lover's painted dream.
Благодаря талантливой Елене Шведу за прекрасный портрет этого любителя лошадей нарисовал мечту.

Thanks for the essential oil consultations provided by *www.oilyrenaissance.com*
Changing the way we look at health—one oil at a time.

Glory to God. May the works of my hands bring honor to the house of the Lord.

Dear Reader:

If you enjoyed this book, please take a minute to help other people find it by sharing a simple review.

Sign up on my website for new release notification so you will find out about the next book as soon as it is available. Also, for any contests or giveaways—join me at http://www.susancount.com/

Hearing from readers encourages me to keep writing. E-mail a comment: susancountauthor@yahoo.com

Please like Susan Count at http://www.facebook.com/susancount where I post only horse related videos.

I'm also on Twitter: https://twitter.com/SusanCount

And Pinterest: https://www.pinterest.com/susancount/

SELAH'S
Painted Dream

SUSAN COUNT

CHAPTER ONE

*T*ime to go already?" Selah groaned. "Do I have to?"

Grandpa checked his jeans pockets for his truck keys. "There's more to life than riding Sweet Dream."

She rubbed the black horse's withers. "She *is* my life. I'd rather ride than anything."

"I know, sunshine. Here, I'll take her." He took the lead rope from Selah. "I'll turn her out while you run, get your stuff, and load up."

Selah grasped Dream by the halter and kissed her nose. "You're the prettiest, sweetest, smartest mare ever. I'll miss you so much."

She dashed up the familiar, well-worn stairs of Grandpa's farmhouse and burst into her room. The galloping white horse fabric on the overstuffed cushion in the window-seat reading nook was worn thin. The window overlooked the pasture where her Sweet Dream grazed.

After stuffing her things into her backpack, she paused at the door. She kissed her finger and touched the nose of a paint horse's photograph hanging on her wall. "I love you—always." She sighed sadness. "Where are you, Buddy?"

Her eyes swept the room. This place felt more like her room than her room at home did. Even though she could only be there on weekends, it was where her heart's treasures were stored. Her grandmother's horse books, which had been left to Selah, and the Breyer horse collection covered every shelf. She was convinced someday they would want to make a model of Sweet Dream. Someday—when they were famous. Selah shut the door gently on her dreams.

Tossing the pack weighed down with books into the truck, Selah leaned her head back, sighed with great contentment, and drifted off to sleep.

Grandpa shook her awake when they arrived home. "You sure play hard to sleep that sound. Makes for a quiet trip."

"Thanks for the ride, Grandpa. You gonna come in for dinner?"

"Not this week. Katie's making my favorite."

"Pulled pork." Selah beamed. "That's really nice."

"I love to eat. I'll see you Friday." He leaned over and kissed the top of her blonde head.

"Bye, Grandpa. You're the best grandpa ever."

"Are we celebrating?" Selah's mouth watered as the scent of warm rolls drew her into the house. Her family gathered around their special occasion, dining room table. She ruffled the hair of both her little brothers as she walked around the table.

Dad tugged off his tie and gestured for her to sit. "Indeed we are. I have some incredible news to share. Things have worked out better than I could ever have hoped or imagined."

Selah returned his grin. Life was already amazing. She spent nearly every weekend at Grandpa's farm riding her horse.

"Your mom and I didn't want you to worry so we didn't mention it, but the company I work for went up for sale right after the New Year." Selah's dad sat tall with his broad shoulders back. He rested his carving knife beside the platter of roast duck. "It looked like I would be unemployed by summer. But great news!" He smiled at each one in turn. "An offer's already been made on the company, and the prospective new owners have promised jobs to any of us willing to move to Austin."

"*Move?*" Instant panic struck Selah as her world exploded like a crystal horse figurine crashing onto the stable's rock floor. Pins and needles pierced her skin like the shards from the shattered crystal. Her eyelids fluttered closed and she leaned into the privacy they provided while she fought for air and denied reality.

Her little brother, Davy, had an equal but opposite reaction. His freckles seemed to explode all over his face at the idea. "Move! Yay! We'll live near Uncle Christopher and Anderson."

She flattened her potatoes with her fork. "What about my friends? I'm a teenager now. I have a life!"

Dad flashed a puzzled look. "There're girls your age in Austin. I promise."

Mom chimed in, "Plus, great music. Great food. Great countryside."

Selah narrowed her blue eyes as disbelief caused her mouth to drop open. Shock stuck in her throat.

"We're lucky this opportunity came up because most of the jobs I'm qualified to get would have moved us to Georgia or California. Without a job, I can't feed you or feed that horse of yours."

Selah leapt to her feet. "It takes Uncle Christopher *three* hours to get to the farm. Can't you find a job here?" Her pale-pink fingernails dug into her fists.

"That's enough, young lady." Dad wagged his fork at her.

Her mouth pulled into a pucker. "Moving would wreck my whole life."

"I know it's a shock, but it's the best thing for the family."

"I can't move to Austin. Not now, not ever!"

Dad rose from his chair, slapped his napkin on the table, and towered over her. Both her brothers gawked at her outburst. A stricken look contorted Mom's face as she wrapped herself tighter in her thin sweater.

Selah frowned at them. Her jaw tensed and locked.

Dad pointed up the stairs. "Take your disrespectful behavior to your room."

In her head, Selah bellowed her outrage. She raced up the stairs as her tears gushed. She wanted to slam the door off its hinges. "This can't be happening. How could they do this to me?"

She pressed her back against the closed door and slid to the floor. Tilting her chin up, she thumped her head against the wood with each word. "Horrible. Awful. Terrible. Wicked. Mean. Cruel."

Curled into a ball on her bed, Selah flicked her gaze to the door when she heard a soft knock and then back to staring at the carpet. After a minute, the knob turned, and the door opened just enough for Davy and Michael to slip inside.

Davy approached the bed. "Selah. I made you a sandwich." His voice rushed out quiet as he held a paper-towel wrapped bundle up to her. "Peanut butter and strawberry jelly—your favorite. I even cut the crust off for you."

A sad smile lifted her mouth's drooping corners. "Thank you—you're the best. I'm not very hungry, but it was so sweet of you to make it."

With total concentration, Michael set a superhero plastic cup on her table. "I poured you some milk. Almost all by myself. Davy helped."

"All by yourself—for me. Thank you."

Michael grinned and rushed to hug her. "Don't be sad, Selah."

"You can keep your horse in my room in our new house." Davy rested his hand on her shoulder as Michael shifted to occupy her lap. "Michael and I talked about it—didn't we, buddy?"

Michael nodded with great enthusiasm. His soft red hair brushed her cheek.

"Michael and I can share a room so there will be a room for your horse."

"Guys, I love you for trying, but Sweet Dream can't live in a house."

"Sure she can." Davy scrunched his face in puzzlement. "We can get her special rubber shoes so she doesn't hurt the floor."

Michael tilted his head to look up at her and offered his helpful idea. "She can use the backyard for a potty."

With that, a smile from her heart spread across her face. "You're the best little brothers—ever." She reached out to Davy and drew him into a hug.

A few minutes after the two mini superheroes headed off to get ready for bed, another soft knock pled for her attention. "Selah, honey. May I come in?"

She forced herself to roll off the bed. She peered around the door but kept it safely between them.

"I brought you some dinner. Mac and cheese." While her mom's sweet tone comforted Selah, her eyes looked red, puffy, and troubled.

Selah reached to take the glass of milk and the foil-covered plate. "Thank you. I'm not sure I can eat anything, but it does smell good."

"Try and eat a little something."

She nodded.

"You're not a child anymore, and we should have told you about your dad losing his job. We were so worried and then overwhelmingly relieved when this new job opened up that we didn't consider how much this would affect you. We feel terrible we didn't prepare you better for the changes coming our way." Mom tilted her head and searched Selah's eyes.

"Moving is the worst news ever. It changes my whole life. I won't be able to ride Dream as much, and that will wreck my training schedule. I wanted to be able to compete at nationals this year with Jordan. I won't have any friends at school—none."

"We don't have good choices. Come here." After a long hug, Mom said, "I've got to get the boys tucked in. Things always look better in the morning."

One of a hundred horse posters that plastered the walls and back of her door slipped off as her mom eased the door shut. Selah restuck it to the door. She lifted the foil-covered delivery and sniffed the mac and cheese. It enticed her enough to take a bite, but one was enough so she covered it back up and set it beside the sandwich.

She'd no sooner changed into her pajamas than a firm rap landed on her door. The door opened a crack, and a disembodied hand entered holding a pink bowl.

6

Curious, Selah tiptoed to the door and peered into the bowl. Ice cream. Vanilla ice cream—her favorite. Chocolate and caramel syrup swirled across the snowy mound, and whipped cream topped the whole deliciousness. "Thanks, Daddy."

When she lifted the bowl, the arm disappeared, and his head appeared. "You're welcome, sunshine. We love you. Keep your eye on your blessings as we go through this challenge, okay?"

Her mouth full of sweetness and her eyes full of sadness, she nodded. If only the cold in her mouth would soothe the stabbing pains in her heart.

The next week passed in a blur. Selah could tell by her quiz grades, she hadn't heard anything in her classes. No matter how she tried, she couldn't seem to force herself into the present. Maybe because she knew how much her reality would hurt and she couldn't face it. She wanted her happy self back. Being mad at everyone and everything was no fun, but she felt powerless to stop.

On Friday when Grandpa came after school to pick her up, his neighbor, Miss Katie, rode with him.

What's she doing here? Selah grumbled as she shoved aside Grandpa's barn coat and muck boots to make room in the back seat. Katie's silver hair was the longest Selah had ever seen on an

7

old woman. Usually, it was tied in a tight ponytail, but today, it hung in flowing ripples.

Selah's eyes shifted from the back of Grandpa's head to Katie's as she followed their conversation about Katie's sheep and her artwork all the way home. *Grandpa is laughing at everything she says, and she's not said a single funny thing yet. Nauseating. Hello, remember me?*

"I love our driveway, Grandpa," Selah interrupted the gaiety in the front seat. "I always feel like we've driven into my secret hideaway. The rest of the world doesn't exist when I'm here." Pine needles sprinkled the roof of Grandpa's house nestled among the trees.

He eyeballed her in the rearview mirror, and Katie glanced briefly over her shoulder. They both smiled at her, and then at each other.

He stopped his old Chevy and tore himself away from his conversation with Miss Katie about planting radishes long enough to say, "Selah, go get settled in." He twisted in the seat to look back at her. "All the animals will be excited to see you. They think life's pretty dull without you around."

"I could stay forever." She waited for a response, but they were already talking about rosebushes. The moment Selah opened the truck door, Skunk erupted into a barking frenzy. "I'm the life of the party." She threw her arms wide to wrap the black and white Aussie dog in a hug. Then a little louder, she said, "I miss them. I wish every day I could be here." A quick glance toward Grandpa told her he wasn't paying any attention.

His arm draped across the back of the seat, and his focus rested on Katie. "I'm going to drop Katie at home, and I'll be back after a while."

Selah's shoulders drooped, and she caught a gnat before she thought to close her mouth. As Grandpa drove away, she stood where he left her and fished the gnat out. One hand rested limply on Skunk's head. "Will you look at that? He drops me at the curb like I'm baggage. How did my life go from perfect to rot overnight?" She scuffed the toes of her pink boots in the dust as she trudged to the house. "What just happened here?"

Pearl met her at the door and meowed a soft welcome. Selah dropped her pink pack on the wooden kitchen chair and scooped up the cat, tucking its softness under her chin. Closing her eyes, Selah relaxed into the rumbling purr. "Grandpa's letting you in the house now. Took ya long enough. Told ya he was a pushover." Long, cream-colored fur, the same color as Selah's hair, clung to her hand. Coaxing Pearl onto a cushion, Selah stepped out onto the porch and lifted her voice. "Dream!"

Hooves pounded as Sweet Dream cantered in from the far pasture. Selah ran to meet the black mare. Throwing her arms around the horse's neck, she breathed in the spring-grass scent of her. "It's not dark. We have time for a ride." Faster than a pan of fresh-baked cookies can disappear, she tacked up and rode out.

As the absolute beauty of spring in The Canaan Grasslands lifted Selah's troubled heart, she urged Sweet Dream into a canter. Her joy in the moment soared.

They eased to a stop on the knoll where she'd first seen Dream almost a year ago. The trapped horse would've been devoured by buzzards if Selah hadn't found her when she did. "It makes me so happy to be here. I can almost forget what is about to happen to me." She leaned forward onto the saddle pommel and slipped her hands around the horse's neck as far as she could reach. "To us."

Maybe it was the fresh air. Maybe it was because when she rode she was in the moment, but as she enjoyed the meadow, all things became very clear in her mind. Selah had a plan.

"Grandpa. He's my ticket. He'll do anything for me." Her fingers fidgeted with the reins. *I talked him into a cat. Who but me could've talked him into keeping Sweet Dream?* She moved a hand to cover her heart. *When he sees how hurt and upset I am, he will surely suggest I come live with him. It's the only way this can work.*

When she rode back into the farmyard, she checked for Grandpa's blue truck in the driveway. "Not back yet! Good grief." After pulling off the saddle, she rubbed the mare dry with a towel.

Selah's empty stomach drew her toward the house. She sniffed the dribble of milk in the carton and checked out a wedge of moldy cheese. "Guess, it's PBJ." But the loaf of bread smelled suspiciously sour.

When the truck rumbled into the yard, she popped out to greet Grandpa. "Nice shirt," she called to him. "Pearl snaps. Aren't you fancy?"

"Katie got it for me. I like it. You have to change things up sometimes or you get stale."

"Katie buys you shirts?" She put on her best are-you-kidding-me look, but he ignored it.

"Bet you're hungry," he called, gathering the grocery bags. "Did you get in a ride?" He settled the bags on the counter and dug through them with total concentration. Flipping the cap off his always neat, white hair, he pulled out and dumped a bag of frozen vegetables and chicken in the frying pan.

"I'm starving." She handed him the dried basil. "We had a super ride. She is awesome. She behaves beautifully even though she hasn't had any work during the week. Imagine how great we could be if I could ride her every day?"

Grandpa squinted at her and tilted his head. A wrinkle appeared between his eyebrows.

He knows I'm up to something. Somehow, my moving to the farm has to be Grandpa's idea. She whispered in Pearl's ear. "We can't make him suspicious."

He slid the hot food to their plates, but before he sat down, she rattled on. "It's so great to be here with you, Grandpa. Do you miss me when I'm gone?"

"Sounds like a loaded question. You've only been gone five days, but yes, I miss you."

She flashed her sweetest perfect-teeth smile as she settled into her spot at the kitchen table. "Dad says our family has to move to Austin." She dropped on him what she hoped was a shock bomb.

"Yes, I knew it was a possibility."

Her voice shot up an octave. "You knew?"

"You'll like living in Austin."

The milk in her glass sloshed onto her hand. "How could I when it's so far from you and the farm?"

"You're going to have to find a way to make the best of it."

"Why can't I live here?"

Grandpa choked on his rice. "A girl your age needs to live with her family. Can you see the look on your brothers' faces if you told them you were not moving with them?"

Ouch. "I hadn't thought about that." *They would be upset.* "But girls my age go off to boarding school and into training camps for the Olympics."

"I'm too old to raise you. You're a lot of work, you know." Grandpa put a forkful in his mouth and stared at her.

"I sure would miss them. But you need somebody here with you." She waved toward the refrigerator. "There isn't even any food."

"I don't need much, and Katie feeds me dinner most nights."

She's the problem. "Katie feeds you." Selah glared in bewilderment. *You don't need me?*

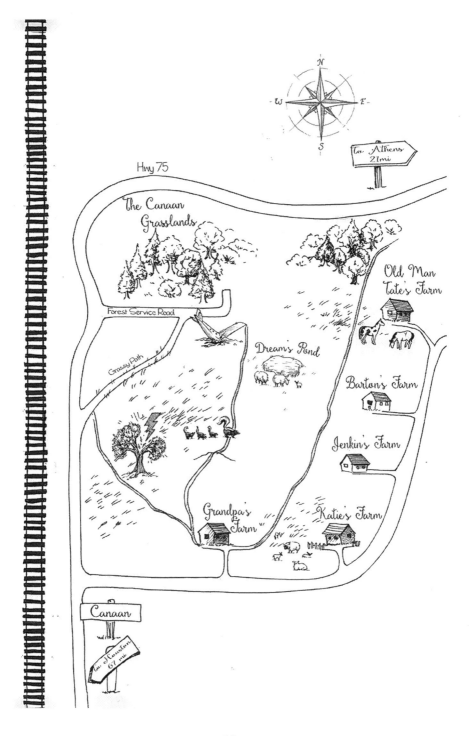

CHAPTER TWO

*T*he morning sun was barely awake when Selah rode Dream into The Canaan Grasslands. There had to be something she could do to make Grandpa see her moving to the farm was a terrific idea. If he warmed up to her idea, then her parents would, too. "If it weren't for Katie, he would have suggested it himself. But Katie's not going to stop me."

Sweet Dream's head flew up, and she spun sharply. Ears pricked forward, the mare snorted in alarm, shaking Selah in the saddle.

Selah gripped both reins and made tight contact with the bit trying to steady the horse. She stared down the service road. It dawned on her something was brushing along the crowns of the trees and coming fast in their direction. A red-and-white plane lurched and wobbled toward them as it snapped the tops off the small pines.

Dream made the decision to save them both when she bolted and plunged into the forest. She lunged through the thick brush, making a beeline toward the farm. Selah crouched low and hung on as if her life depended on it. She yowled as her knee impacted a tree.

Behind them, trees cracked and splintered. Then came a thud and the screeching crunch of metal. Quiet returned to the forest.

Dream skidded to a stop at the top of a deep ravine and trembled. Selah braced in the stirrups, so she didn't fly over the mare's head. Even through the western saddle, she could feel Dream's heart pounding. The mare's sides heaved with exertion. Selah kicked her feet free of the stirrups and vaulted to the ground. She winced as she landed and her knee buckled. Rubbing her painful knee, she clutched one rein. Dream pranced around her, flipping her nose and blowing hard.

"Easy, girl. Easy." Selah turned with the horse, speaking soothing words, but staying clear of her clomping hooves. She needed to calm the horse, and talking sweetly wasn't working. Her feet tangled in the brush. She fell beside Dream, jerking on the bit, for which she would apologize later. She narrowly missed getting her hand stomped on. Leaping to her feet, she had to take control before Dream became completely unmanageable. She asked Dream to execute her groundwork exercises. She yielded the mare's hindquarters, asked her to go forward then backward. Now sidestep away and circle around. As soon as the mare's head lowered, Selah positioned the horse by a log and climbed into the saddle.

They retraced their steps toward the service road. "How did you not break a leg galloping through here?" She grimaced at the number of deep holes they had passed in their mad crash through the woods. Dream picked her way through the fallen branches of a dead tree in the last fifteen feet to the road.

As they stepped into the road, Dream's head flew up, and her eyes bulged showing the whites. Selah sucked in her breath.

The plane lay tilted and crumpled against a giant oak. One mangled propeller and a hunk of aluminum littered the ground behind it. A forest service emblem was stamped on the tail, and FIRE in white letters emblazoned its fuselage.

"I've been telling Dad I need a cell phone. Nobody listens to me." She stared at the contorted mess. Leaping off Dream, Selah got a painful reminder to be more careful with her knee. She unhooked one rein from the bit and ran to the plane, leading the horse behind her.

Dream swerved from side to side trying to turn back.

"Dream! Stop it." Selah popped the rein to get the scared horse to snap to attention. "We have to see if anybody's hurt."

The horse snorted, pranced, and tried to pull away.

"Okay, forget you!" Selah sprinted away from the plane, looking for a place to tie her mare.

As she dashed back to the plane, her nose burned and her eyes watered. Fuel dripped from the wing.

A man larger than Grandpa lay slumped over the controls.

She cupped her hands on the window and around her mouth. "Wake up!" she yelled.

Selah tried to open the door, but it wouldn't budge. Bracing one foot against the plane, she yanked. The door creaked and groaned as she wrenched it open. Something smelled like smoldering wet newspaper. From her first aid training at the equine therapy ranch, she knew it was dangerous to move someone who'd been in a wreck. She had a quick decision to make. Risk hurting him worse or take the chance the plane would catch fire while she went for help.

She unbuckled his seat belt and grabbed the man's arm. She pulled, but he didn't move an inch. She gripped his shoulder and shook him as hard as she could. His head rolled to the side and thumped on a bar. A gash on his forehead oozed blood into his thick brown hair and dripped it onto his uniform.

Jumping back from the plane, she yelled again, "Wake up!" She sniffed distastefully as the smoke in the cab thickened. While she wasn't good at equations, she knew airplane fuel plus fire equaled an explosion. She looked at Dream as if the horse would know what to do.

Sweet Dream slung and stomped one hoof as she flipped her nose in rhythm. Her level of anxiety clearly transmitted to Selah that Dream thought they should get out of there. Trusting the horse's instincts could save her life, but what about the man?

"God, show me what to do."

Looking frantically around, Selah spotted a pack behind the seat labeled Survival Kit. Fingers shaking, she pulled it out of the plane and dug through it. She didn't know what she hoped to find, but she was pretty sure the candles wouldn't help. Neither would the insect repellant, but under the silver thermal blanket hid a coil of nylon rope. She held the rope up and showed it to Dream, flexing her muscles like she'd already won the victory.

After a deep breath to gather her courage, she reached around the man's waist with the rope. Her hands trembled as she tied a knot. Slipping backward from the plane, she lost her balance, and her sore knee ground into gravel. She jumped up and raced toward Dream with the end of the rope.

The horse's eyes widened with fright, and her nostrils flared.

"Pull yourself together, Dream. I can't do this without you." Making a quick loop, Selah hooked it over the saddle horn. "Easy, easy. Whoa. I'm counting on you."

She stumbled back to the plane. The fuel smell stung her nose, a small flame sputtered under the plane's belly, and smoke billowed around the nose cone.

She wiggled the rope, asking the mare to pull it taut. "Whoa! Steady."

Sweet Dream snorted and flipped her head.

"I don't care what you think. Just do it." A low crackling urged her to hurry.

The horse pulled backward. The man slid from his seat. Selah tried to hold his head in her hands. He flopped and hung out of the plane like a sack of feed, one foot twisted and wedged under a foot pedal. "Whoa!" she yelled to Dream.

She leaned way over him. First tugging on his boot and then his leg, she jerked his foot free, leaving his boot entangled in the pedal. With a deep breath, she reached farther and grabbed the dashboard transmitter. She pushed the button and yelled into the radio. "Help! Hurry. We're on The Grasslands' service road."

No one answered.

"Back, Dream, back!" When her arm brushed against hot metal, Selah jerked it away and scrambled to get to her horse. Leaping into the saddle, she backed the mare faster, dragging the unconscious man across the gravel road, through the drainage ditch, and along the road's grassy shoulder.

Still, there was no sign of anyone coming to help. Tugging the loop off the saddle horn, she cried out, "What do I do now?"

It feels like I should go. She wheeled Dream to a sandy path leading to the highway and urged the horse into a run. They easily jumped a log and galloped on. Selah crouched low on the mare's neck so tree branches wouldn't sweep her from the saddle.

The mare puffed hard and sucked in great gulps of air. Whitetail deer bounced off into the thickets, making way for the jet-black bulldozer barreling more like a locomotive than a horse. An explosion rocked the woods behind them, and fear propelled them forward.

"Run, Dream, run!"

At last, Selah spotted cars traveling on the busy two-lane highway that intersected with the service road. Just before they got to the road, she slowed the mare at the edge of the woods and slid to the ground. A logging truck sped by. Yanking her rain slicker from the saddle, she waved down a passing car.

An old Buick slowed and stopped. The window cranked open inch by inch. A little face, framed with short silver hair, looked out. "Are you okay, dear?"

"Yes, but can you call the police and the doctor and the firemen?"

"Well, yes, dear. I have a cell phone my son got for me." Waiting for the woman to dig around in her purse was a lesson in patience for Selah. HURRY!

Another car stopped. Leading Sweet Dream, Selah ran to him. "Please call the police and the firemen." Before she even began the story of what happened, the man dialed 911.

"Operator, I'm on Highway 75 about seven miles north of Canaan. I'm giving the phone to a girl who has an emergency."

Her hands shook as she fumbled the phone to her ear. "A forest ranger crashed his plane on the service road in The Grasslands." She all but screamed at the 911 dispatcher. "We got him out, but then we heard his plane explode. Please hurry." She swallowed hard.

Then they waited. She stood on the roadside, holding Dream's reins. She wiped at the grime on the rearing horse shirt her mom had given her for no reason, hoping it would come clean enough. The burn on her arm smarted. Through the rip in her new Wrangler jeans, Selah fingered a pebble embedded in the flesh of her knee, prying it out and causing it to bleed.

The nice lady offered her a cookie from a Christmas cookie tin. The man in a suit leaned on his black sedan, still on the phone with the 911 operator. Cars slowed as they passed, and the people gawked.

When Dream nudged the cookie tin, the lady smiled, selected another cookie, and offered it to her. Dream's lips worked the cookie off the lady's hand, and it disappeared. "My horses used to like coconut cookies, too." The lady giggled when Dream smacked her lips.

"You had horses?" blurted Selah, shocked.

"Oh yes. I was a rodeo queen once. I led the entry parade, every night of the fair, on my beautiful barrel horse."

Speechless, Selah tried to imagine the little old woman on a horse until her attention shifted down the road.

In the distance, the comforting whine of sirens drew near. Relief flooded Selah. Tears filled her eyes and rolled down her cheeks. Then her legs wouldn't hold her up any longer. She sank to the ground and sobbed.

The sheriff knelt beside her to ask questions. More police cars barreled onto the road shoulder. He pointed down the road and told the officers, "You can get to The Grasslands service road from Highway 75, three miles north."

An ambulance stopped, and a medic checked on Selah before driving after the caravan of police cars and fire trucks after she assured him she was okay.

The radio attached to the sheriff's shirt squawked with progress reports.

"Selah, I've called your grandpa, and he is coming to get you. I'm leaving a deputy here with you, but I'm going to the scene. The advance patrol has spotted the smoke and should get to the ranger soon." He rubbed the top of her hand. "Thank you."

She realized she wasn't holding Dream's reins. "Dream!" she screeched, and her fists clenched as she spun around in panic.

"She's all right, dear." The tiny lady in the print-flowered dress held the reins in one hand and the nearly empty Christmas cookie tin in the other.

Grandpa's truck eased off the highway with Katie's rickety trailer rattling behind it.

"You can't be serious, Grandpa? A stinky sheep trailer."

"Glad you're all right, Selah." He opened the squeaky pipe gate to the stock trailer.

"Dream would rather walk home."

"That would give you plenty of time to think about what's coming out of your mouth." He frowned.

Walking to the lady by the road, Katie hugged her. "How can we ever thank you for being here with Selah?"

Grandpa turned to the small woman. "Yes, thank you."

"Ed?" She stepped closer to him.

His forehead wrinkled at the lady. "Do I know…? Fran? Fran!"

She threw her arms around him. Fran hugged him tight and smiled through her tears. "How nice to see you after so many years." She pulled back from him. "You look wonderful. As handsome as ever. I was passing through the area. Ever since my husband passed, Nellie's been after me to move back and help her make pies at her bakery." She tilted her head, and her smile lingered. "I like the idea of moving home. We could pick up where we left off so many years ago."

Selah's head pivoted from Fran to Katie. *This is getting interesting.*

"We need to get Selah home, Ed," interjected Katie, pulling on his sleeve.

He released Fran's hand, but he gazed into her blue eyes. "Katie, this is Fran. She's an old friend."

"Nice to meet you." Both ladies acknowledged the existence of the other.

Then Fran turned her back on Katie and talked to Selah. "I'm so happy to have met you. Love your horse. May I come watch you ride sometime?" She smiled. "I think we could be great friends."

Selah nodded yes, but her tongue stuck to the roof of her mouth.

Fran twirled in slow motion back to Grandpa. "Call me, Ed. We should talk. I'm staying with Nellie." Clutching the cookie tin, she backed up a step before dropping her chin and fluttering back to her car.

Hm…Selah's mind raced with possibilities. *Cookie-tin lady likes Grandpa.*

He reached for the lead rope. Selah didn't release it until he gave it a firm tug and her a firm look. He led Dream to the trailer.

Dream sniffed and then snorted at the trailer floor. One hoof pounded on the floor planks. After thoroughly testing it, the suspicious horse stepped into her sheep-scented limo.

Even as Katie took Selah by the hand to lead her to the back seat, Selah's eyes followed Fran. *If I could pick a girlfriend for Grandpa, she would love horses and want me to live at the farm.* With a weary smile, Selah laid her head back and allowed exhaustion to win.

21

Selah woke as they arrived at Miss Katie's pale yellow house. White shutters shone, reflecting afternoon sunlight. Sheep filled her pastures, and chickens clucked, roaming free in the yard. The rooster sat atop the picket fence surrounding her kitchen garden. A china teacup, overflowing with birdseed, hung from the nearby flowering crepe myrtle.

"I'll be only a minute, Ed." Turning to Selah, Katie asked, "Does chicken noodle soup sound good to you?"

Selah shrugged and looked away. "I'm not really hungry."

"You're still in shock." Katie reached over and touched her arm near the spot Selah burned on the plane. "I've got just the thing to take the sting away, and tomorrow, you won't even notice it. That should help you sleep better tonight. I've got a big bandage for your knee."

Selah drew her arm away and covered the quarter-sized burn protectively with her hand.

"I'll bring some lavender oil for Sweet Dream, too. All this has got to have unsettled her. I use it on my sheep when there is a thunderstorm approaching."

Selah longed for Katie to go away—poof—disappear, but she stood beside the car looking expectantly at Selah. As the pause lengthened, Selah felt Grandpa watching. "Thank you," she said politely.

The sheriff was parked in Grandpa's gravel driveway when they got home. "I know it's been a long day, Ed, but I have a question for Selah."

"She's pretty worn out."

22

"I'll be quick about it." The sheriff removed his hat and rolled it around in his hands. "Selah, how did the ranger get so far away from his plane?"

"I looped the rope over the saddle horn, and Dream pulled him out of it. I guess I was scared and didn't realize how far we moved him. Did we hurt him? Is he dead?" Her face tightened, and tears rushed past her resolve. "I'm sorry. I was trying to help. I didn't know what to do."

"Don't you cry, little darling—you did great." He slid his hand onto her shoulder. "He is alive *because* of you. Glad to know why he was tied up like a goat."

She noticed the corners of his mouth turn up ever so slightly before his seriousness returned.

"The plane exploded, which I think you guessed, and it burned to a crisp. If you'd left him in it when you went to get help, we'd be having a funeral this week." The police radio in the car crackled and buzzed. "The grass caught fire and burned about three hundred yards downwind and another one hundred feet the other way. If you hadn't dragged him across the road… Well, you did the right thing. And the Good Lord must have been looking after you because, if you and Dream had been there when the plane exploded, shrapnel would've hit you. Several metal pieces were sticking out of trees."

"Did the ranger get hit?" asked Grandpa.

"The medics took him away with a hunk of metal embedded in his thigh. But he was unconscious, and the surgeon removed it before the ranger even knew it was there."

"So, he is okay?" She brightened.

"He is, thanks to you and the wild-thing you call a horse. He will be in the hospital for a while with the injuries he sustained in the crash. But he'll make a complete recovery, I'm told."

"Dream was amazing. I couldn't have done it without her." She nodded and stifled a yawn.

"I think Selah's had enough for one day." Katie put her arm around Selah and tried to usher her into the kitchen.

Selah stiffened and edged closer to Grandpa. *What does Katie care about me?*

CHAPTER THREE

*I*t seemed every time Selah put the phone down it rang again! "This phone is bugging me, and I need to groom Dream. Her tail is totally tangled."

Grandpa rustled and repositioned his newspaper. "Since Cooper released your DVD, everybody in town has been talking about you and Dream. Long before you made the paper this morning. I suggest letting the answering machine get it."

"The paper, too? I knew it was on Facelook."

"Aren't small towns great? There's a big article, with pictures even, about the rescue yesterday." He held the paper to show her. "I went to the bakery in Canaan, and Nellie told me every stranger who stopped asked if this is where Sweet Dream lives."

"Did you bring me donuts, Grandpa, or did you go to see your rodeo queen?" She bit her lip to keep the smug smile from bursting into a triumphant one.

"Donuts behind you. Special for you—chocolate covered with rainbow sprinkles."

A mouth full didn't slow her down. "So was Fran there? She was so good with Dream. And Dream really liked her."

"Fran was there, and we talked a bit over coffee." He folded the paper and dropped it on the side table.

Selah tugged the giant bandage from her sore knee. "You never told me you dated a rodeo queen."

"A long time before I saw your grandmother ride in the exhibition." He stood and stretched. "You need to mind your own business, young lady."

"You know I'm no good at that. Silly Grandpa." She poked his belly with her knuckles as she teased him.

"Your grandma's friend, Laura, saw the article. She called to tell you your grandma would be fussing at you for taking the risks you did helping the ranger, but she'd also be proud of your bravery. She said your adventures bring back memories of an exciting buggy ride when she and Grandma Mary were your age. She wants to come ride with you."

"Awesomesauce. I can't wait." Selah plucked a glazed donut hole from the white bakery bag.

"Those are mine." He rescued his donut holes.

Popping it into her mouth before he could grab it, she mumbled, "Caroline called while you were gone." She swallowed the donut with a dramatic gulp. "She went with her dad early today, giving West Nile vaccinations at the fairgrounds. They stopped at the café for a late breakfast. Did you know it has a sandwich plate called the Sweet Dream Special? They even wrote it across the café window."

Grandpa rolled his eyes and tossed a donut hole into the back of his mouth.

"Caroline said people who stopped to eat asked the waitress about Dream. Everyone wants to know if Dream will be in a movie. Dr. Steve says Dream is good for the economy of Canaan!"

"Good grief. This is ridiculous. I can't get even get a piece of pie at the café without a crowd gathering. People are wondering if I am going to erect a sign at the farm gate saying Home Of Sweet Dream." He folded the top of his white donut bag and set it between them. "Why is it you amp up the voltage around here so much? I'm quite fond of my quiet life. I'm too old to deal with the chaos that follows you and ambushes me."

"I'm sorry, Grandpa. I know it got a little crazy for you, but it'll die down. You'll see." She pinched the corner of the donut bag and ever so slowly eased it closer.

"You would think grown people would have more important things to talk about than the antics of a horse."

"Like, what's more important than talking about Dream?" She grinned, popping a donut hole into each cheek.

"If you will try to stay out of the paper and out of my donuts, everything will settle down," he assured himself as he snatched his bag back.

That was before Selah's riding mentor, Mr. Cooper, called.

Asleep on the couch, Selah jumped when the phone rang. Grandpa lay his book on his lap and activated the speakerphone. She rolled over and pulled the cushion over her head.

"Ed, we're getting wagonloads of fan mail for Selah and Sweet Dream."

When she heard the horse trainer's voice, she sat up clutching the brown velour pillow to her chest.

"Ha!" Grandpa laughed and held his side like it hurt. "Is Selah making you famous? I've no sympathy for you, Cooper. I can't even have a cup of coffee in town without fending off people's questions about them. At first, it was funny, but now, it's plain obnoxious."

Selah stuck her bottom lip out as far as possible in her best pout.

"They have captured people's hearts, and folks are calling every day to ask for an autographed picture. What do you want me to do, Ed?"

"Wish I knew. I never thought it would get this wild. Plus, they're on the front page today after Selah and Dream pulled a forest ranger from his plane before it exploded yesterday."

"From a plane? Wow. Maybe they should make a movie. This has taken on a life of its own. I've made lots of demo training DVDs, and I've never seen this before."

"It would help if she could stay off the front page of the local paper. We're not prepared to deal with this. Selah's parents are less than thrilled with the media attention." Grandpa scratched the top of his head and glanced over at her. "I was just telling Selah it will all blow over soon. I'm dreaming, aren't I?"

"I'm afraid you are. People think she's the cutest thing in pink they've ever seen. They're a sensation."

Selah showed every tooth in her mouth and alternated bouncing one shoulder then the other as she mouthed a celebration song.

Grandpa rotated in his chair to her as he switched off the phone. "You heard the man. It's going to be crazy for a while. Guess we better get used to the idea."

"I can't get over that there's been more calls for our filming session than for some of the big names they've featured on the show. More even than that country western superstar you're so crazy about." She threw up both her hands with her fingers spread wide and leaned toward him. "Doesn't that just blow your socks off?"

He rubbed an itch behind an ear. "Yeah. It takes a lot to impress me, but yeah. And he's my favorite singer, too."

Selah's cat leapt up on the couch cushion, climbed to the arm, and then onto the back where she sashayed the length of it and stepped onto the windowsill.

"Pearl gets to walk on the furniture now?" Selah untangled her long legs and started to the kitchen. "How did she charm you into being in the house?"

"You can thank Katie for Pearl's status change."

Selah shrunk inside, and her happy spirit withered. "I've been trying to make Pearl a housecat forever, and you always said..." She gestured like it was his turn to tap dance.

"Never going to happen. I know. I know. And look at us now. She wasn't any good at being a barn cat anyway."

Fuming, Selah gritted her teeth as she left. She stood in the middle of the kitchen and couldn't remember why she'd come.

When the phone rang again, he picked it up before it finished its first ring. "It's Caroline again, for you," he called to her.

She hurried back to him, took the phone, and put her hand over the mouthpiece. "I told her about having to move. She's trying to cheer me up. She wants me to move here so we could start high school together in the fall."

He picked up his book and hid behind it.

Every muscle on her face frowned at him through his book, and she forced herself to sound cheerful. "Hi, Caroline. What's going on?" She listened, nodded, and smirked. As she set the phone down, she bent toward him.

"What?"

"Caroline was in the beauty shop getting her hair cut short-short today. Fran was there. She told everyone you were the most handsome cowboy on the circuit and she should never have let *you* get away." She leaned even closer to him and stared into his eyes. "All the ladies think you're going to dump Katie now that Fran is back. They say she's set her sights on you and she's not letting you get away twice."

Grandpa waved her away. "People should mind their own business and stay out of mine. That includes you."

"Aren't small towns great?"

He looked over the top of his glasses at her. "I'm going to check the mailbox."

It'd been too long since she'd eaten so Selah smeared strawberry jelly on top of peanut butter on crackers and popped a whole one into her mouth.

"Didn't we just have lunch an hour ago?" Grandpa elbowed his way through the door into the kitchen balancing the mail. "Package for you."

"Me?" She hefted the big awkward box onto the island countertop. "It's from Miss Laura."

"That's nice." He sorted his mail, pitching the political flyers into the trash. As he opened the bills, she reached for the scissors and cut the tape on her package.

"What in the world?" She lifted a strap attached to a dingy, cloth-type mesh. "Why would Miss Laura send me a dirty horse blanket?"

"It's to keep flies off. I'd agree with you, though, it's odd."

"She wrote me a letter. Want me to read it to you?" Selah glanced at a picture and slipped it behind the letter.

"Sure." He tugged open another piece of mail.

"'Dearest Selah, I wonder what you will think when you open this and see I've sent you a dirty and very old flysheet. If it looks ratty to you, it's because it's had a hard life.'

"What I think? I wish she'd sent me a new one. And Miss Laura is on the quirky side." Selah's brows pulled together as she pondered the strange gift.

"You got that right." Grandpa wadded up a piece of paper and lobbed it toward the trash.

"'Let me explain,'" Selah continued reading. "'Once upon a time, it belonged to Dream's great-great-grandmother—our beloved Illusion. It's in rough shape because as much as she hated flies, she hated flysheets more. She could never be convinced they were for her own good. I've never used it on another horse. I could never bring myself to wash away the last of her sweat and hair.'"

Selah fingered the flysheet. "Aw.... How sweet is that? She saved this all these years."

Grandpa's eyes shifted to Selah as she read.

"'I like to think it still has her scent. It takes me back to the days when your grandma and I were young and life was all about horses. Illusion is where it all started. I've never known a horse to be so devoted. Watching them, you'd think they shared brainwaves. It never looked like Mary cued the horse, but the mare did amazing things for her. They were magnificent together.

"'When her career as a reining horse wound down, we turned Illusion out in the pasture where she was born. She lived the sweet life with our other broodmares. Mary hoped to raise another

Morgan horse just like her. Of course, while she blessed us with many adorable foals, there could never be another Illusion.

"'In the last few hours of her life, she fought to stay with Mary. Mary cared for Illusion with amazing tenderness. Even in pain, Illusion never had anything but the sweetest disposition. In that final moment, Illusion lifted her head to stare Mary in the eye. The quiet nicker she fluttered as life left her body was a tender goodbye.'"

Selah pursed her lips and glanced at Grandpa, who seemed to be staring at a spot on the wall. "You were there, weren't you, Grandpa?"

He nodded. "She was thirty-three. Nice long life for a horse. Still, your grandma wasn't ready to let her go. Second worst day of my life."

"I can't think about what it would be like to lose Dream." After a long silence and a deep breath, she continued reading.

"'So you see, this ratty old flysheet may not look like much, but I think it holds her essence. While it pains me to part with it, it seems only fitting Sweet Dream should have it. Maybe some of Illusion's spirit is infused in the fabric and will rub off on Dream. Maybe some of Illusion's heart, strength, and determination will sustain Dream when she needs it.

"'I promise to bring Illusion's granddaughter, Harmony, to ride with you soon. I can't wait to witness Sweet Dream's reaction to seeing her dam again after so long.

"'Love and blessings from your honorary Great-Aunt Laura. Isn't that a wonderful title I've given myself? P.S. I also wanted you to have a copy of this picture.'"

Selah angled the picture so Grandpa could see it before returning to the letter.

"'Fred Classan took it—we were just kids then. He's a famous photographer now, but you can see he had a gift even then. I think

32

it captures your Grandma Mary's spirit. Her joy. Her love. Her fun side. We are showing off our wild socks. It was taken at the reining event that made your grandma famous and changed her whole life. Notice Illusion is not wearing a saddle or bridle. That's me by Illusion's head. I look a mess.'"

Selah's voice quivered. "'In the crowd behind us. See the cowboy holding his hat in his hands? He hadn't even met Mary yet, but you can tell from his quiet smile and the light in his eyes he'd just fallen in love. Can you tell who it is?'"

She peeked at Grandpa over the letter. Tears rushed from her eyes to be caught up by her smile. "It's Grandpa." She hurried around the counter to hug him around the waist.

CHAPTER FOUR

I feel like I woke up a hundred times last night. I had the same nightmare over and over again. I moved to Mongolia, and I would never see Sweet Dream—ever again." Selah tugged on her boots. "I need to ride."

"Here. Put this in the barn on your way." Grandpa pushed the flysheet box toward her. "Be careful, okay?"

"We'll be fine, Grandpa. If you had a horse again, you could ride with me. We should get Buddy back. It'd be so much safer than riding by myself and more fun, too."

He waved her off.

"Come on, Skunk. Let's go play—while we can. Before my family drags me off to the other side of the world."

Skunk responded with an "aarall" and an enthusiastic bark.

"Feeling a little melodramatic this morning, aren't we?"

She bristled. "You don't understand."

"You best learn to deal with it." He pointed a finger at her. "And watch your tone with me."

"I'm sorry. My insides feel like a knot. Come on, Skunk."

With an invitation to go, Skunk bounced beside the horse, barking her delight. The sun was high over the treetops. Golden light filtered through the branches, and the rising moisture shimmered with energy. Dragonflies zipped and darted in pursuit of a meal. Dream flipped her nose when a dragonfly rocketed under her chin. Selah threw her arms wide. "How can my parents take this away from me? How can Grandpa not see what a terrible mistake he's making?"

Dream walked with long, steady strides following the trail. Skunk took a less direct route. She crisscrossed the trail behind them searching for something that might like her to chase it. Her efforts were soon rewarded when a rabbit jumped and revealed its hiding place. The chase was on!

A quiet rustle right next to the trail made Selah jump. Dream reacted in the same moment by sucking backward. Slithering through the leaf litter was a thin snake. A snake so colorful it looked like a piece of dropped jewelry—until it moved again. It lifted its head above the grasses and arched it one way and then the other.

Selah seized up with fear. Her fingers tightened on the reins, causing Dream to tense, too. "Black and yellow, black and red—oh, what is the rhyme?" She gripped the pommel with her other hand to steady her trembling.

The snake twirled itself around the trunk of a bush and climbed.

"Red and yellow, that's it. Red and yellow kill a fellow." She backed the horse. "It's a coral snake, Dream." Selah shuddered. "We need to let it be."

Dream stomped her hoof, firmly indicating her willingness to take care of this little colorful problem. Selah moved Sweet Dream further away from the snake, off the trail, and skirted around it.

As she picked up an easy canter, Selah's heart soared. She flung her arms high and out to the side. "I believe I can fly." Lifting her face to the sun, she let her song of praise rise to the heavens. She eased deep into the saddle, and Dream obediently stopped. They stood on the knoll where Selah first saw the black shadow that turned out to be Sweet Dream. She breathed deeply the glory of the morning.

"This is where I belong. With you, Dream." Her arms wrapped around the mare's neck. "I can't move to Austin. I need to be here, or...my soul will just die." She stroked the softness of Sweet Dream's neck. "The farm is such a part of who I am. My parents don't get it. Grandpa is busy with Katie." Her eyes glazed as she stared at the grasses, but her mind was so occupied she saw nothing. "We gotta do something, or we could lose everything that matters."

Another movement caught Sweet Dream's eye. The horse's ears alerted long before Selah clearly saw the furry black something waddling down the trail. She stood in the stirrups to see better. One long, black-and-white streak fluttered toward them. Behind it came about a dozen smaller tails held up like flags.

"Uh-oh! It's a whole skunk family! I want to see the babies better. Wonder how close we can get before she sprays us?" Selah decided a wiser course of action was to move off the trail—way off—since the procession obviously owned the road. About that time, Skunk, who'd given up chasing the bunny, spotted the furry family.

As Skunk gathered momentum, Selah yelled to deaf ears, "No, Skunk!"

It didn't slow her down. Bounding past them, the dog charged headlong into a heap of smelly trouble and discovered she'd made a serious judgment error.

Defenses deployed, mother skunk and all her darling skunklits turned tail and scurried back the way they had come. Selah's nose clogged. Dream snorted and shook her head.

The pitiful dog yelped and rubbed her face in the dirt. Dropping her shoulder to the ground, pushing with her hind legs, she moved forward at a furious pace. Her nose plowed the dirt. She flipped to her other shoulder all the while yipping and yelping. A monstrous dust cloud rose from the thrashing, yowling dog.

"Ah, poor Skunk." Selah and Dream could only watch the dog writhe in torment. "Let's take you home, Skunk." Selah reined her horse around and trotted out.

Skunk seemed torn between the need to save her nose by burying it underground or the terror of being left alone with her stench. When she rocketed past Selah, her skunk perfume wafted behind her. Selah buried her own nose in the crook of her elbow trying to shield herself and not breathe. Her eyes watered, stung, and blurred. Dream sneezed and held her head close to the ground as if she'd like to bury herself, too.

Grandpa knelt in the dirt, peacefully planting basil in the kitchen garden when the bedlam blew into the yard. "Selah's here." He scratched his head and chuckled. "My home remedy for boredom."

The smile on his face revealed his tender heart for her. Then the smell bowled him over.

He dragged the garden hose into the grass next to the blue dish soap and a giant bottle of vinegar.

Selah whispered to Dream as she un-girthed the saddle. "That will keep him home with us. So much for his 'date' tonight."

The next morning, a chestnut-brown metallic truck rumbled into the yard. Skunk, normally the farm doorbell, raised her head but whined in defeat as her nose sank to rest on her paws. Grandpa had bathed her in "everything under the kitchen sink", trying to clear the air. Her full fur collar gleamed a brilliant white. Still traumatized from her skunk encounter yesterday or maybe from the repeated baths, Skunk retreated under the deck and refused to be consoled.

Selah's riding coach slid out of the truck as Selah trotted in from her morning ride. "Miss Jordan," she called. "What are you doing here?"

"Cooper gave me a few days off so I'm on my way to Houston to spend some time with my parents." Even though it was a day off, Jordan was still dressed in boots and jeans that had seen a lot of arena dust.

"A day off? Is he sick?"

Jordan laughed. "He works harder than any of us. He was saddling his second colt of the day before I finished my coffee." She shrugged. "The training center is my life. I'd rather be working horses than anything, so I try to keep up."

"I wonder what would have happened to Dream if Mr. Cooper hadn't offered to train her. Grandpa was ready to stuff her in a dog food can."

Jordan doubled over with her hands on her knees. Her ponytail hung across her face as she roared with laughter. "Come on. Help me unload your mail," she said when she caught her breath.

"My mail. How crazy?" Sliding from the saddle, Selah tied Dream to her post.

Jordan dragged stuffed canvas bags from the truck and passed one to Selah. Lugging them to the porch, Jordan asked, "What is that stench?"

"Skunk, met a real skunk yesterday. First thing Grandpa did was call Queen Katie for advice." Selah crossed her eyes. "If he'd asked me, I could've told him to use ketchup. Instead, he poured every concoction Queen Katie suggested on poor Skunk, but she still stinks."

Jordan picked at the knot tying the bag closed. "I hate to break it to you, but ketchup is an old wives' tale."

"She smells like the girlie lotion store in the mall with the undertone of dead fish and rotten garbage."

"I would try some hydrogen peroxide," Jordan suggested.

"He keeps wanting to put something else on her, but every time she sees him with a bottle, she scurries farther under the deck. I don't blame her."

"Who is Queen Katie?" Jordan raised her eyebrows, making her brown eyes look huge, and waited for Selah to explain.

"Grandpa's 'neighbor'. More like girlfriend if you ask me, but I was told to mind my own business."

"A little competition, Selah?"

"Everything is different. He's late to pick me up. He used to always have my favorite foods, and now—he's out of everything." She waved her arms around. "He never used to answer the phone. He didn't care who called him. His answering machine would fill up with messages." She gestured like she was conducting a crescendo in a symphony. "Now every time the phone rings, he runs to answer it. It's always her, and he dashes to her house to help her with whatever."

"Aww. I think it's sweet."

"Sweet? My family is moving to Austin. If I go with them, I'll never see Dream. If Grandpa wasn't always running out the door, I could try to talk him into my living here." She made a sour face. "But then I'd never see my family. Lose-lose. Either way, I lose all my school friends and my favorite P.E. coach and my horse and my life." Selah slapped her hands on her hips. "Moving is evil."

"Why don't you move Dream to Austin?"

"Because she lives here for free. Plus, Grandpa still trims her feet. My mom said our family can't afford to board a horse and pay a farrier every six weeks."

"It does get expensive. Let's change the subject. Fan mail, for you." Jordan reached into one of the mail bags, pulling out a big handful of letters, and offered a bunch to Selah. "I try to be grateful for this day. You can't change or control the future."

"That's what Grandpa said, but an old girlfriend of his moved to town. Fran likes horses. She might change everything."

"Maybe a better thought would be to make friends with Queen Katie."

Selah scoffed at Jordan's suggestion as she flipped through a stack of letters. "Here is one from Florida. One from Arizona. Idaho." She plopped into Grandpa's favorite cushioned chair.

Jordan settled into a chair on the porch beside her and read, "'Dear Selah and Dream. My name is Betsy and I have always wanted a horse, but I live in the city. My favorite episode of the Cooper series is the one of you and Dream.'"

"Here's one from Tyler, Texas. 'I look out my window every morning to see if a lost horse has come to take me away,'" read Selah.

"This girl says she is practicing all the round pen exercises with her sister in case she gets a pony for her birthday."

Selah smiled. "Ah, that's a cute one. 'My name is Julie. This is a picture of me and my horse, Flame. Please send me a picture of you and Sweet Dream. Thanks. P.S. I love your cream-colored hair. Mine is dark brown, but I got it cut just like yours. It looks great, even after wearing a riding helmet.'"

Jordan slapped Selah's leg with a stack of letters. "I'll have to talk to Cooper, but I think we can set you up with a blog and a Facelook fan page off Cooper's site. Then you could share with your fans some of the things you're doing with Sweet Dream."

"My own blog? And a fan page? My parents will hate the idea, but all the girls at school will be so jealous!"

"It would help cut down on the calls and bags of letters if your fans have a way to communicate with you on social media."

"This is so fun! I love being important."

"Enjoy the ride for now. I need to get going. My mom's making lunch." Jordan gave her a quick hug and hustled on down the road.

Selah waved goodbye and pulled another wad of letters from the bag. She read silently.

You're not as hot as you think you are. Anybody can ride a horse after it's been trained for them. Your sugar-sweet smile makes me sick.

She pitched the letter onto the porch table. "Ouch."

The phone rang in the house, and she dropped the grooming brush and dashed to answer it. "Hello."

"Is this Miss Selah?"

"Yes, sir."

"Selah, I'm Fred Classan. Is your grandpa there?"

"May I take a message?"

"You may. I'm an old friend, and I called to offer to take some pictures of you with your horse."

"Thank you. That's very nice, but my grandpa is taking care of it."

"My last name is spelled C-l-a-s-s-a-n. Tell your grandpa I called, okay?"

"Yes, sir, I will. Goodbye."

Muttering to herself, she headed back outside to finish grooming Dream. She snapped her fingers. "Classan! He's the one who took the picture Miss Laura sent. Hum."

Pearl entangled herself in Selah's ankles and intercepted her tromp to the barn. "You're utterly irresistible kitty-pie, and you flaunt it." Selah scooped her up and held tightly to the little cream-colored purr. "You worked some kinda magic on Grandpa. Even though he gives Katie all the credit—I know it was you. Teach me your secrets, will ya?" She rubbed her nose in the cat's fur. "He said you couldn't be in the house, and yet here you are. Will you put in a good word for me and help me work the same deal? I'm not about to butter up Katie." She crushed the meow to her chest and carried her out to the barn. "Everything has gone wrong, Pearl. What are we gonna do?"

Selah squeezed her cat with one more hug and slid Pearl to Dream's back. Pearl nestled on the mare's rump, tucked her paws under her, and watched Selah work combing out the horse's bushy tail. Dream's ears swiveled, but wherever Pearl wanted to sit was tolerated by Sweet Dream.

"Hi, Grandpa! I did the dishes and swept the kitchen floor."

"It's nice to have that kind of help around." Grandpa set his hammer on the porch. He stood transfixed, watching his girls.

Dream's head sank lower as she drifted off to sleep. Pearl's eyes flickered closed, and her face rested on her paws. Selah hummed a quiet melody as she worked the twists out of Dream's tail. He slipped into the house and a moment later came out with his camera.

As the camera clicked, Selah looked up and smiled for him. *He's changed his mind. He wants me to live here. You can see it in his eyes.* "You missed Jordan. Did you see the porch?"

Turning, he threw up his hands and gestured toward the bags stacked there. "What in the world? How did I miss those?"

"Miss Jordan brought loads of mail they'd gotten at Cooper's ranch since the video was released."

"Wow, what an impressive pile!"

He pulled a letter and read, "'I hope you fall off and break something so you know what it feels like.'" He made a face at the letter. "That's a bitter little person. If this is fan mail, they can keep it."

"Yeah." Selah grimaced but quickly recovered. "I've learned not to open the ones with no return address."

"We're going to need to get a bank loan for postage if you try to answer half the people who've written to you."

"Not to worry, Grandpa. Most people included an email address, and Miss Jordan says Mr. Cooper can have his webmaster set up a blog for me."

"A blog?"

"Like a diary on the internet."

"Oh." He tilted his head and raised his eyebrows. "Girls used to keep locks on their diaries. Now every private thought is posted on the internet."

"Welcome to my world. Miss Jordan said she would help me figure it all out." Selah gestured to a growing pile on the porch table. "I'm not going to answer my hate mail. Why do people who've never met me hate me?"

"Don't bother trying to understand why people hate, sunshine. Respond with the overflow of the kindness and love that lives in you."

"Can I borrow your shredder?"

Grandpa laughed and rubbed Sweet Dream's withers. "Cooper told me we need to get a professional photographer out to get a good portrait done. They will overlay a signature and then you will be able to email it to folks."

"Oh, I almost forgot. A man called while you were in the front pasture. He said he wants to take pictures of me and Dream. He has a funny last name. C-L-A-S—I wrote it down."

"Fred Classan?"

"That sounds right. Isn't he the one Miss Laura mentioned?"

"That's him. We were buddies growing up and had a lot of good times before he became 'The Famous Fred'. He used to hang out at all kinds of horse events where he took pictures for a living. He got a shot of me riding the buckin'-est horse in the string at a rodeo in Wyoming." He sighed. "Then Classan got married, moved to Nevada, and we lost touch. He wrote a book on wild mustangs featuring his photographs. Excellent work—it catapulted him into prime time. What a coincidence he would call today," muttered Grandpa, shaking his head.

"You rode bucking horses?" Selah's mouth hung open. "No wonder Fran thought you were amazing."

Grandpa seemed lost in his own thoughts, and her comment breezed without notice. "I wonder if he's coming to Houston. He is incredible with a camera. People all over the world pay him big bucks to take pictures of their horse."

"If he's in Houston and he wants to take our picture, then I should stay here. I'll call Dad right now and maybe catch him before he leaves the house."

"School tomorrow. Back to the real world. You best finish up here. Your dad's on his way."

"Grandpa, you know I don't want to go!"

"I know, sunshine. I like time with you, too."

I knew it. Selah strolled into the house and flipped her things into her backpack. A smile crept across her face. *Katie's no match for me. I'll think of ways to keep his mind off her.*

CHAPTER FIVE

Selah shouldn't let them get to her, but sometimes, when her brothers weren't being adorable, they were totally gurr.... They chewed with their mouths hanging open and left their clothes all over the bathroom. Five-year-old Michael's hair dusted the floor as he peeked into her room, under the door. Davy knocked on her door every time he passed. When she opened it, no one was there. His deep-blue eyes peered at her from behind the hinges of his door.

"Leave me alone! Both of you."

Ultra-curious about the photographer, she powered on the computer to research him before breakfast. When she plugged Fred Classan into a search engine, a long list of links popped up. Some threads showed his most recognized photographs. Lots of links were articles and recognition for his accomplishments and his outreach ministries. "He's really famous."

On one site, there were pictures of the president of Russia mounted on a massive bay stallion, a princess from England dressed to follow the hounds, a sheik from Saudi Arabia standing in his tent doorway, his hand resting on his prize Arabian mare. "She's majestic."

Scrolling down, she "oohed" at a picture of a beloved first lady trotting her horse in Central Park, New York with her two children mounted on ponies beside her.

A knock at her door. "Davy," she growled under her breath. She didn't look up from the screen until her dad's deep voice bellowed, "Selah! Time for school."

"I'm coming." She tried not to sound annoyed.

Selah scanned the eighth-grade crowd surging into the front door of the school, to find her best friend. Running to catch up with Vanessa, she could hardly wait to tell her about Mr. Classan. As she was about to shout out, Vanessa leaned to Jade. "Some cowboy puts her riding lessons on TV, and she thinks she's so hot! How lame is that?" Vanessa's ringlets swung with the energy of the conversation.

Heat rushed to Selah's face. Locked in the moment, her lungs refused to breathe.

Their mutual friend, Jade, chimed in, "It's just not right how she throws all that in your face. You'd never guess such a goody-goody could be so hateful."

Her friends walked on to class without noticing her. *Why are they talking that way?* Selah moved through the morning in a zombie state. Everyone seemed to have a friend, but her. The exchange between Vanessa and Jade repeated in her head like a scratchy recording. *Feels like I just had my face bit off. I wonder if I should go wipe off the blood.*

She took refuge in the girls' restroom and stood staring into the mirror. *I always listened when she talked about the Welsh pony she brought from Connecticut and her "dressaaaaage" lessons. I was her only friend when she first moved here! Everyone else thought she was snotty. Now she thinks I am.*

The bathroom emptied, and Selah realized the clanging in her head was the tardy bell. She tried to slide, unnoticed, into a chair at the back of the classroom.

Her teacher pointed at her. "See me after class."

When the bell rang on her last morning class, she looked at her blank notebook. Why would she have notes when she didn't hear a word the English teacher said? She waited by the teacher's desk until the room cleared.

The teacher closed and locked her desk drawer. "Don't let it happen again."

"Yes, ma'am." As she left the classroom, she glared at the clock and cringed. It was their lunch period! *I will have to face them in the cafeteria.*

Watching the blur of classmates from just inside the cafeteria entrance, she prayed to be invisible.

Jade's dark eyes glared at her as she interrupted Selah's trance. "Why are you staring at me? Are you comin', or what?" Jade turned away and tossed the question over her shoulder. Without waiting for an answer, she settled next to Vanessa at the table the trio always claimed.

"Like you care," Selah answered to Jade's back as she eased into the cafeteria line. "Your hair looks terrible, ya know," Selah muttered. "It looks like someone poured jet-black shoe polish on your head."

A girl in skinny jeans stood in line in front of Selah. She twisted around. "Did you say something?"

Selah shook her head.

When she cast a discreet glance at Vanessa and Jade, a wave of nausea passed through Selah. Then their eyes met, and Vanessa fluttered a feminine wave before she gave her attention back to Jade. Pain rolled over Selah.

She set her tray down and sat her little bruised self on the bench. Looking across the table at her two friends, she waited for some indication she was welcome. None came.

Her friends glanced at each other then studied her. "So..." Jade twirled and pulled on a black hair spike. "How's the farm?"

Hearing the sarcasm, Selah was afraid to trust her voice. She forced herself to smile and nod.

The girl in skinny jeans set her tray down next to Selah. "Can I sit here? My friend is out sick today."

Selah nodded. The other two girls took big bites of their hamburgers.

"I'm Amanda. I'm in your P.E. class." She slid onto the bench seat. "I saw the TV episode with Cooper. That is the coolest."

"Oh, thanks, Amanda. It was amazing. His training techniques are the best."

"You're going to be famous. That's so great."

"Right. Because it's so great to get hate mail from people you've never met. Yup. So great." Selah mashed a green bean into pulp. "If you watch Cooper, you're into horses."

"I am. I ride at Pine Hill."

"I know that barn. Do you have a horse or do you just take lessons?"

"I work there on weekends, and I board a Welsh pony I got for Christmas. Her name is Golden Glory."

"A palomino, I guess?"

"So beautiful she takes your breath away."

Vanessa interrupted, "I have news! I'm going to visit my aunt in Connecticut. I've outgrown my Welsh, and we're going shopping for a Warmblood Dressage horse from Germany. Daddy says it's time to take my dressage to the next level."

"Wow, awesome." Selah leaned in and tried to look more interested than she felt.

Commotion broke out when the bell rang and everyone scrambled to get to the next class.

Selah usually walked with Vanessa and Jade to class after lunch, but when Selah put her tray up and looked for them, they'd left her. She moved closer to Amanda, grateful her new friend kept talking.

"We should ride together sometime. I bet Miss Cindy, she owns the barn, would let my dad borrow the farm horse trailer. I've always wanted to ride in The Grasslands. Or you could bring Dream to our barn show this summer." Amanda took Selah by the arm. "We could have so much fun together. I can't wait for you to meet my horse. Gotta get to my locker before class—we can talk more later."

As Selah turned into the open door of her next class, she caught Vanessa out of the corner of her eye talking enthusiastically. Jade's smug smile covered her face when she spotted Selah watching them.

The next morning, the thought of going to school made Selah's stomach hurt. "Mom, I feel sssssick." She curled up on her side under the covers and drew her knees to her chest.

Her mom laid her cheek on Selah's forehead. "You don't have a fever." Drawing back, she studied Selah's face. "What's really wrong?"

"Besides moving?" She punched her pillow then curled it in half to tuck under her neck. "I was behind Vanessa and Jade yesterday, and they were talking about me."

As Mom feathered her fingers through Selah's hair, her lavender scent brought a sweet comfort. "So what did they say?"

"That I was a snob since all this has happened to me with Dream going to Cooper's and all."

"Have you done anything to leave them with that impression?"

"No!"

"Well, maybe they misunderstood something you said." Her mom rubbed tiny circles on her back.

Selah's voice squeaked as she whined, "I don't know." Her forehead wrinkled and her lips puckered. "She and Jade act like they hate me."

"They're your best friends, and you need to talk to them about it. Go into the conversation with a heart of forgiveness and not a chip on your shoulder."

"Why? I'm moving. My life is ruined." She closed her eyes and pulled her pillow over her face.

Selah arrived at school as the bell rang. She dashed for her first class. Vanessa and Jade strolled the hallway, arm in arm, and they flutter-waved. Selah leaned toward Vanessa. "I need to talk to you at lunch about something important."

Vanessa's mouth held a sneer, but she nodded. Everyone hurried to class.

At lunch, Vanessa and Jade didn't wait for her again. She didn't see Amanda. The smell of pizza enticed her into the cafeteria. The girl in front of her picked up the last carton of chocolate milk. By the time she finally got her slice of extra cheese, her friends had already finished eating. Selah tried to make some small talk. "So, is anything new with you guys?"

"Besides getting a new horse. Nah. What else matters?" Vanessa scooped her bangs from her eyes with two fingers.

"I kinda need to talk to you. You won't believe what's happening to me."

"Figures—it's all about you. It's always *all* about *you*." Vanessa stood holding her tray.

Selah's bite of pizza turned toxic in her mouth. "Well, you're gonna love this! I'm moving to Austin." She untangled her legs from the bench and snatched up her tray.

Jade flashed an oversized, triumphant smile, and then walked off with Vanessa without even a backward glance.

Selah flung her school pack onto the bench by the back door.

"How did it go today with Vanessa and Jade?" Mom peeked in the oven, releasing one of Selah's favorite smells. Gooey, melting cheese.

Not even homemade macaroni and cheese could save her day. "Pretty terrible. The only thing worse than moving to Austin is being in a school where everybody has decided they hate me." Selah tromped up the stairs. "Not that anybody cares," she muttered under her breath and locked herself into her room. "Friday's coming, and Grandpa will come for me."

CHAPTER SIX

Selah made it all the way through the week only to find out the ground shifted under her feet. "What do you mean Grandpa can't pick me up?" She exhaled a huff.

"Grandpa has a date." Selah's mom brushed flour off her hands. The laptop on the counter played contemporary praise music, but Selah didn't have praise for anything right then.

"Oh great."

"Don't be like that. Your grandma passed away almost eight years now, and Grandpa needs companionship."

Selah doodled a stick horse in the flour dust on the board. "He doesn't have time for me anymore."

"You need to think about someone besides yourself. Katie makes him happy."

"And me miserable." Selah scowled as she garnished her drawing with a mane and tail. "The photographer is supposed to take my picture with Sweet Dream tomorrow. Is that canceled?"

Mom eased open the oven door to peek at the snickerdoodles. "Your dad is driving you to the farm after dinner."

Even as cinnamon tantalized Selah's nose and made her mouth water, her mind locked onto changing her world. "If I could go to school in Canaan and live with Grandpa, then he wouldn't be lonely anymore."

Mom slid the cookies from the oven. "Very thoughtful."

"We could get the newest phone, and I could use an app to be at our family dinner time every night."

Mom transferred the cookies to a glass plate and offered one to Selah.

"I'd get to start high school with Caroline instead of a crowd of mean faces. Every three-day weekend—I could come to Austin. It would be just like I was in boarding school—only better because I'd be with Grandpa." She watched for any sign of agreement. "Please think about it."

"What makes you think Grandpa wants to deal with your drama?"

"Because I'm his sunshine." *I have to figure out how to convince him he needs me there. Then he can help me convince Mom.*

Selah poured her nighttime glass of milk and dug in the cabinet for graham crackers when she heard Grandpa's boots thump up the porch steps.

"Hello, sunshine." He stepped in the kitchen door. "Don't eat all my graham crackers." He teased.

She hugged the package to her chest and warned him away with her eyes.

"Where's your dad?"

"He says hi, but he couldn't stay." A smile graced her face for him. "I'm so glad to be here, Grandpa. You have no idea how bad it's been at school."

"Why? What's going on?"

"Everybody's saying I think I'm important after being on Cooper's TV program."

"They're just jealous." He waved off her concern. "You'll make all new friends when you move, anyway."

"I'm going to pretend you didn't say that."

Grandpa handed her a white box. "Fred will be here first thing in the morning."

"Yum." Peeking into the box, she smacked her lips. "Brownies are my favorite." She slid the package of grahams across the counter toward him.

"Anything chocolate is your favorite."

"You look pretty sharp. Did you have a date?" She savored the treat. "It's weird to have your grandpa dating. Fran?"

"Never you mind."

"Come on, Grandpa. Details," she mumbled with her mouth full. "Did Fran send me the brownies?"

"Katie made the brownies for you."

Selah set the box down. Suddenly, she wasn't hungry even for chocolate.

"Something wrong?"

"They have nuts. I'm allergic to pecans."

"You're safe then. Those are walnuts."

"I've had enough anyway."

His mouth tightened. "Did you bring clothes for your photo shoot?"

She nodded.

"Pink. I would guess."

Selah shrugged, tilted her head, and her charm returned with a smile. "And my hat and dress boots. You'll be so proud of me." She dug into her bag and whipped something behind her back. "Pink socks—wait for it—they *match!*" She giggled as she held them high for him to see.

"Say it isn't so. I think my heart stopped." Grandpa thumped himself on the chest.

"Oh, Grandpa, you're silly. I wish we could be together all the time." She tossed her socks into her bag. "I've been working to get Dream ready."

"As you should."

"I gave her a bath. I didn't have time to redo her pink highlights because Dad had to work late, so it was nearly dark when we got here."

"I'm glad ah that. Fred would think I'd lost my mind—streaking a horse's mane with pink."

"She needs her pink. We need to be color coordinated if we're going to make the equine fashion news."

He unloaded his pockets onto the counter. "Katie's coming over to help you get ready in the morning while I do the last-minute touchups with Dream."

She straightened and pulled her shoulders back. "I don't need any help. I'm not three."

"I asked her to come. She has an artistic eye, and I think her feminine touch will be helpful."

Her chin jutted forward. "She wears tops with big flowers in neon colors."

His dark eyes warned her. "That's enough, Selah. What's gotten into you lately? You flip from your delightful little self to, well, let's just say, I'm not liking your tone."

"Me?" she whined. "What's gotten into you?" She plopped one hand on her chest and covered it with the other. The daggers in her eyes melted into teardrops, but anger spewed from her mouth. "You used to like having me here on weekends, and now I'm in the way—of more *important* things."

He pointed at her. "I'll say again. Watch your tone or zip it."

"Sorry. Sorry. I don't like me much right now. Everything in my life is wrong, and I don't know how to fix it."

He cupped her chin in his hand. "Sometimes there is no fixing it. Troubles in life reveal the cracks in our hearts."

Her shoulders sagged as her eyes brimmed with tears. "I'm sorry. I don't mean to be like this."

Later, as she slipped into her pink, pony-print pajamas, her attention was drawn to her devotional notebook. She traced an *S* in the dust on the cover.

The next morning her best intentions were overwhelmed by her frustrations. Selah tiptoed to the head of the stairs, careful to avoid the creaky boards, and listened to the whispers in the kitchen. When Katie's laughter drifted up the stairs, it met Selah's hard heart. *He'd want me here if it weren't for her.*

She held the wooden rail as she eased down. Katie leaned comfortably with both elbows on the counter, smiling up at Grandpa like it was her own kitchen. So engaged in telling Katie something, he didn't notice Selah until she cleared her throat.

"Ahhhum. Good morning." Selah popped open the refrigerator. Holding the bottle of orange juice by the neck, she swirled the half inch of juice around. "Is anything in here fit to eat? Not sure this juice can pass the sniff test."

When Grandpa didn't even seem to hear her, she frowned her hurt feelings at Katie.

Pearl wound herself around Katie's legs and purred. Selah scooped the cat up. "Traitor," she muttered into the cat's soft ear as she whisked the purr away and deposited her outside.

Grandpa topped off his coffee. "Fred will be here in less than an hour. Get the beautification process started. Katie can help with your hair, and she is going to put a little makeup on you."

Flashing a quick smile, Katie ran her hands under her long hair and slid it over her shoulders. "That's why I'm here so early." She glowed like a child with a new box of crayons.

"I'll bring you up a smoothie in a few, Selah. Katie, can I bring you something?"

"I'd love some tea. Orange spice?"

Selah angled away, hugged Pearl, and mocked Katie silently. *I'd love some tea.*

Katie followed Selah up the stairs, chattering all the way. "I've brought some sculpting pencils and a set of pink powders for blush and shadows." She spread the contents of her orange bag onto a cloth atop the bed. "Sit here for me." She dragged a small, straight-backed chair closer to the bed. Then she swept Selah's hair back from her face and clipped it out of the way. "Your hair is such a lovely, soft blonde and is a nice flattering length." She applied foundation to Selah's face. "What a precious picture of you and the paint horse. I remember him. He was a treasure."

"He was Grandpa's exhibition horse. I'll never understand why Grandpa got rid of Buddy."

"It was a painful time for your grandpa. I remember the silly horse acted like a big puppy. He went up the porch steps and almost trailed you into the house once. Your grandmother followed the both of you everywhere with a camera. There was a darling, darling picture your grandma took of you kneeling beside a saddle on the ground. The horse put his head right by the saddle as if he was trying to tell you how to get that thing on him." Katie highlighted Selah's brows with a soft brown pencil. "I seriously expected the horse to grab it in his teeth and throw it over his shoulder onto his back for you."

"I loved Buddy. I wish he was still here." Selah twisted a tissue into a bow. "You knew my grandma?"

"Of course. We were neighbors. We were both artists, so we had a lot in common. My husband and I used to play bridge with your grandparents."

"And now you're Grandpa's girlfriend?"

Katie pulled back from her work, cocked her head, and looked puzzled. "That explains why you're so upset." Katie assessed her work and brushed a light blush on Selah's cheeks. "Your grandpa and I are very good friends. Sometimes it's nice to have a friend to spend time with."

"Just friends?"

"It's been lonely for both of us. We share a lot of warm memories and have a great time together."

"I didn't know Grandpa played bridge."

"Only because your grandma loved the game and he'd do anything for her." Katie smiled like she was enjoying the memories. "Your grandma was a wonderful hostess. She loved people—by feeding them."

Katie brushed and arranged Selah's hair. She fashioned a ponytail at the nape of her neck. Then taking one section, she twirled a pink ribbon into it. Wrapping the ribbon section around the ponytail holder created a sleek, feminine look. Katie stepped back and admired her handiwork as she fussed with a couple rebellious strands.

Grandpa edged open the door with the toe of his boot and handed in a cup of hot tea and a smoothie. "How's it coming?"

"Just perfect," Selah said.

"I'm glad you two are getting to know each other better." He pulled the door closed.

After a minute of smoothie and tea sipping, Selah blurted what she was really thinking. "It feels like Grandpa would rather have you here than me. If Grandpa doesn't want me here when my family moves to Austin, I'll hardly ever see Dream. That hurts." She sucked in her breath—had she really let those words fall from her heart?

"Oh, that's not true at all." Katie leaned closer to look in Selah's eyes. "I'm sorry that would even cross your mind. Your grandfather looks forward to your coming. You are his favorite topic of conversation."

But Katie's kind words didn't ease Selah's pain.

"You two done up there? Fred's here."

"We're on our way, Ed." Katie scooped her makeup and styling tools into her bag. "Come on. So exciting—a famous photographer here to take pictures of you. Let's hurry."

Even though Selah heard her mother's reprimand in her head— "Don't be ugly, Selah."—she couldn't seem to help herself. She scrunched her face and lifted her nose at Katie's retreating form.

Selah pushed open the screen door and bristled when she noticed how close Katie stood to Grandpa. Katie gestured enthusiastically about something and laughed like a schoolgirl.

No one seemed to notice Selah had joined them.

Mr. Classan hung on Katie's every word and laughed along as she talked about her baby sheep. *Maybe she'll like him and forget about Grandpa.*

"Oh, Selah, come meet my old friend." Grandpa motioned for her to join them.

Fred rotated to look at Selah. "Wow, except for the hair color, she is definitely Mary's granddaughter."

"Yes, the resemblance is uncanny, and even more amazing is Selah seems to have Mary's natural gift with horses." Grandpa slid his hand onto Katie's shoulder and curved her slightly toward himself. "You fixed Selah's hair just like Mary used to wear hers. Thank you." He walked her to the deck, and they settled into the pair of wicker chairs.

Selah stared after them.

"Let's get started before the Texas heat kicks in." Mr. Classan lifted a huge black camera from his bag and fiddled with the dials.

"Hi, I'm Ginger." The assistant approached. "If you'll come with me, Mr. Classan will want to get some stills of just you. Then we will add the horse." Ginger sat Selah in front of a dark-green leafy bush in the yard, swiveled the stool to put her body at just the right angle, and redirected one of the reflector screens. "Perfect. I love the contrast between the lush green and your hair and outfit."

"I need a new SIM card, please, Ginger." Mr. Classan studied the farm layout through his lens.

"Grandpa says you're famous for photographing wild horses."

"I use the talents the Good Lord gave me." Mr. Classan searched every pocket of his canvas vest until he located his light meter.

"I saw some of your shots online. My favorite is of Mrs. Kent in Central Park with her two children on ponies."

"She was a classy lady. The photo added juice to my career in a big way. The picture alone enabled me to make a down payment on a ranch in East Texas. In the summer, it's a horse camp for kids who have a parent in prison." Mr. Classan moved 180 degrees around Selah. "Maybe you could come ride at the ranch for the kids. Show them some of the techniques you've learned."

"I just ride her."

"That's not what I heard. Cooper is convinced you have the same natural talent as your Grandma Mary. As young as you are, I expect you'll be getting better all the time. If you've a fraction of her talent, you'd be a pleasure to watch. I could've watched your grandma ride her reining horse all day." Mr. Classan snapped his fingers. "Illusion was the horse's name. Her name should have been Hypnotist. Every cowboy in the state, including me and your grandpa, crowded the arena rails when Mary rode." Mr. Classan lowered the camera. "Cooper got you doing liberty work?"

"Yes. But it doesn't usually go like it's supposed to. Dream has a mind of her own. Mr. Cooper is having us do a demo with Jordan at the Trainers' Expo. Not freestyle, though."

"Is he? I'll ask him to set you up to ride for the kids at the benefit for my ranch that Cooper's doing in a couple months. It would blow the kids away. They'd love to hear about your adventures, too. Your grandpa told me about the forest ranger you rescued. The story of the skunk encounter would crack them up. Their lives are much different from yours, so sharing your joy in life can give them hope for their own."

Without a smile in her heart, it didn't take long for Selah to get tired of smiling. *This is work and boring without Sweet Dream.* Skunk wandered to Selah, sat smartly by her side, and tilted her head.

"I think she's smiling for the camera." Mr. Classan snapped the shutter.

"Skunk's a wannabe movie star."

"Let's position her on the other side of you and see if she will put a paw up on your knee."

Ginger maneuvered Skunk, who struck a pose looking adoringly at Selah. Selah grinned back at the dog, but when she looked toward Mr. Classan, his back was to her. His camera pointed at a smiling Katie. Katie sparkled as she smiled at Grandpa, making her look like she'd been covered in fairy dust.

Selah gritted her teeth. As Mr. Classan focused on her again, she said, "You seem to like Miss Katie. She's a widow, ya know."

"She is delightful, and she's smitten with your grandpa. Love brings an element to a photograph that touches you."

"What? No way. She says they're just friends."

"I see things through the camera lens. I'm glad he's moving forward with his life again." Mr. Classan adjusted one of his light reflectors. He peered into the viewfinder. "Something else I see through this lens is you're not happy. The problem for me is it's showing up in the pictures. I've gotten several, more interesting snaps of Katie, in the few I've taken of her, than in the hundred I've taken of you. Could you try to think of something pleasant and smile like you mean it, please?"

Selah cringed. *Dear God, Grandpa says I have cracks in my heart. Please heal my cracks because my love has leaked out and I can't find it.*

Mr. Classan eased closer to Katie, the shutter clicking. When he swung his camera back toward Selah and Skunk, a whirl of clicks followed. "That's marginally better, Selah."

"Mr. Classan? Do you know what happened to Buddy, the paint horse my grandpa rode?"

"No idea." He wiped off the camera lens. "Let's bring in Sweet Dream now."

Grandpa handed Katie a tall glass of iced sweet tea.

Selah said out loud to no one, "I've got to find Buddy. He could change everything."

Grandpa had obviously dragged the riding arena earlier because the sand had a rippled beach-like pattern. Now he sat with his feet kicked out in front of him crossed at the ankles. He looked relaxed and happy chatting with Katie.

While she focused on Dream's canter rhythm, joy shone on Selah's face as they streamed around the arena.

"Nice." From the top of a six-foot stepladder, Mr. Classan followed their movements with the camera. Ginger stood next to him and held an extra camera and a black bag.

A sideways glance toward the porch confirmed her suspicions. Grandpa still wasn't watching. *I'm over here, Grandpa.*

"Wonderful," Mr. Classan said. "Can we pull the saddle, please? I'd like to get some footage of you riding bareback."

Selah dropped lightly to the ground and tugged on the girth. Dream curved her head around as if to help. Ginger adjusted her horse cap to shade her eyes from the bright sun and gave Selah a leg up. As she urged Dream into a smooth, easy canter along the rail, Classan framed his shots.

"Oh, wow. She is Mary all over again," Classan muttered. He made eye contact with Grandpa, and they both nodded knowingly.

Selah took a firmer contact with the bit and applied pressure with her legs. The mare responded by shortening her stride and lifting her shoulders. Selah rode a gentle black wave.

Classan shouted out to Grandpa. "You could ride that canter while you drink champagne." Looking through the lens, he urged Selah on. "Nicely done. Keep it steady."

Loving the energy and showing off just a little, Selah and Dream leapt into a gallop. Dust particles streamed into the air, adding a sunlit twinkle as if the silt were really ice crystals.

"That's not what I meant. Let's not gallop bareback, okay?"

A shadow flashed across the sand directly in front of the galloping pair. In a split second, Dream spooked, swerved, and spun, sending Selah flying in the opposite direction. The mane she gripped slipped through her fingers. The useless reins flapped as the mare bolted and bucked, tearing along the arena fence line.

Selah crumpled in the dirt and lay motionless. Dream snorted and squealed. She raced to get back to Selah's side. The mare dropped her nose to sniff Selah then pushed her with her muzzle. The horse stood protectively over her still form.

With the breath knocked out of her, Selah was only vaguely aware of the commotion. Clearly agitated, the mare pivoted and galloped around the arena.

Grandpa grabbed his training stick as he ran from the porch. He pulled his shoulders back, stood tall, and moved with quiet purpose into the arena. Dream sat back on her haunches, lifted her front feet off the ground, and flipped her head up and down. Her ears flattened.

Classan yelled, "Ed, there is no mistaking her intent. She thinks she has to protect Selah."

Katie ran to the gate. "Ed, please. Fred is right."

"Dream looks like a she-devil." Ginger backed away, then ran for the gate.

Selah groaned. Sweet Dream eased toward Selah and nuzzled her cheek. "Dream, get out of my face."

"Selah, can you move?" Grandpa asked.

"Maybe," she answered faintly.

"Katie, go easy around the outside of the arena but stay a good thirty feet from the fence. If Dream turns to look at you, back away. Ginger, drop a handful of pebbles into your soda can and bring it to me."

"Can you roll under the fence, Selah?"

"My shoulder hurts."

"Okay, scoot. Get as close as you can. I'll distract Dream long enough for Katie to get to you." Grandpa sighed.

"Go, Katie." He gave her a head start then shook the rock-filled can. Startled, Dream charged across the arena, hurling sand in every direction.

Katie bent over as if to hide from the horse and ran to the fence.

Grandpa swung his stick like a windshield wiper. Dream snorted, whirled around, and charged back to Selah. He pitched the rock-filled can under Dream's nose. She swerved and struck at the aluminum enemy, buying Katie time.

Squeezing under the fence, Katie grabbed Selah's shirt in one hand and her jeans' waistband in the other and pulled.

"Get back, Dream," Selah commanded the anxious horse as she rushed the fence. Dream paused and tossed her head up and down.

Katie helped Selah sit up as everyone gathered around them.

The horse reared and pawed the air. The moment her hooves touched down, she bolted and thundered along the arena rail as if a swarm of angry fiery dragons pursued her.

"Are you sure she's not a stallion?" Classan shook his head. "Or maybe a German shepherd?"

"That's the biggest brain fart I've ever seen a horse have." Grandpa ripped his cap from his head and slapped it on his knee.

"She was only trying to protect Selah." Katie examined Selah's shoulder with her fingers. "Dream doesn't understand what happened to Selah. She sensed danger, and her instincts took over. In that moment, she was a wild mare protecting her foal from wolves."

Selah flinched. "It hurts there."

"Are you some sort of animal psychic or something?" Classan asked.

"I do have abilities in that area," Katie answered quietly while probing Selah's shoulder.

Grandpa looked bewildered with his eyebrows drawn together in a deep *V*.

Katie tilted her head and shrugged. "It's a gift."

"Well, ask Dream what happened then because I would like to know what is wrong with the crazy horse before I sell her," Grandpa raged.

Her arm resting across her chest, Selah defended her mare. "It wasn't her fault! Did you see the shadow that went over us? It looked like an airplane... or the reflection of a big bird?"

"I did see a buzzard circling earlier," Katie said.

Grandpa folded his arms. "I didn't see any buzzard."

"Maybe because the only thing you really see is your beautiful neighbor," Classan teased. Everyone waited as Classan skimmed through his shots. "I have a picture showing a shadow in front of Dream's nose. Katie is right—it does look like a buzzard." He showed Grandpa the picture.

"I think Dream had a flashback to when the buzzards were after her. Like the ones people have after they have been to war." Selah grimaced as she shifted her arm.

"Oh great." Grandpa huffed. "A horse with Post Traumatic Stress Disorder."

"Horses have a memory second only to an elephant," Katie explained. "It's entirely possible she remembered her trauma with the buzzards. And fearful horses respond to a threat in one of two ways. Flight or aggression."

"While all that is true, how do you know so much about horses?" Grandpa asked.

"I can't explain what I know. I have an ability to perceive what an animal is trying to communicate without words."

Only Selah's eyes moved from Katie to Grandpa and back to Katie. "Let me talk to Dream for a minute so she'll know I'm all right." Selah eased to the fence. With her head lowered, Dream trotted to her. Selah let go of her elbow long enough to rub the mare's face and slide the bridle from her head. "You were just trying to protect me, weren't you? I love you, too. Don't worry. Grandpa will calm down. He always does."

"Well," Classan said. "We're done here. Glad you're all right, young lady." He snapped the lens cover on and removed the strap from around his neck. "Ed, let me know the dates of the expo Selah's going to with Cooper. I told her I want her to ride Dream in the ranch benefit, too."

"If we still have that horse." Grandpa glanced over at Selah's dirt-streaked face. "Maybe she can show them some fancy dismounts."

As Grandpa finished up with Classan, Katie steered Selah to the house.

"I can do it," Selah insisted, tapping the bathroom door shut with her toe.

Soon it opened without making a sound. Selah peered out.

Katie had settled into a kitchen chair.

"Can I help you?"

"Please."

Katie rose and stretched the shirt over Selah's elbow and off her arm. "Get washed up, and I'll get some oils."

About to object, Selah moved her arm and flinched. "Okay."

Katie lined up several little dark bottles on the table and unscrewed their tops. After dropping some coconut oil into her palm, she then added a few drops of each oil before rubbing her hands gently on Selah's sore shoulder. "Some of these oils are from the Bible."

"They do smell nice. But I don't get how oil is going to help my shoulder."

"You'll see. Essential oils are a healing gift."

"I need one for my heart."

"Aww. That kind of healing takes prayer. I heard you ask Mr. Classan where the paint horse went. Why are you so determined to find him?"

"Because the horse was special, and I'd like to bring him home."

"He was special, and I actually think it's a good idea. If we put our heads together, I bet we can find him."

As Selah realized she was starting to smile, she froze it and wiped it from her face. "I'll find him myself."

Grandpa filled the kitchen doorway. "Selah, your dad's almost here. He's going to take you to get your arm looked at."

"Do you have to sound so happy to see me go?"

"I do hope when you can come back you will be in a better frame of mind. But no, it's not that I'm glad to see you leave. I want to know if anything serious is wrong with your arm."

She cradled her elbow supporting her shoulder. "It's feeling better already. I'm sure it's nothing."

But Grandpa had already turned to Katie. "Hum... Let me guess. Frankincense, copaiba, and balsam fir. Am I right?"

Katie grabbed his shirtsleeve and jiggled it. "You wouldn't be making fun of me now, would you?"

"Dad's here." Selah tried to get Grandpa's attention. "Don't forget, Grandpa, come get me right after school on Friday."

"Let's see how your shoulder is doing by then." He kissed the top of her head. "Bye, sunshine." He opened the fridge, peered inside, and asked Katie, "What's for lunch?"

The smile slid from Selah's face. As she turned to leave, her shoulders slumped, and her feelings crumbled like a crushed leaf.

CHAPTER SEVEN

Selah opened the door to find her life in boxes.

"Glad you're home." Mom taped a box shut, stretched, and arched her back as she got up off the floor.

"Is that where I am?"

"What did the doctor say about your arm?" Mom raised her voice over the racket of Michael chasing Davy around the couch and into the playroom.

"Nothing's broken. Be good as new by Friday. Dad went to the pharmacy to get a sling to support it for a couple days."

"How did the photo shoot go?" Mom dug in her apron pocket full of rolls of colored duct tape and black markers.

"Okay, I guess. I thought we didn't move for another month?"

"Closer to two months, but there's so much to do before the big day. I'm trying to get a little packed at a time to make the move easier. I thought we'd do a garage sale soon."

"You never make any money."

"True, but I always go into it with an optimistic attitude. I put some boxes in your room. Those are for garage sale stuff. The plastic bins are for you to pack things you want to keep, but don't need handy for a while."

"This is the worst nightmare I've ever had." Selah plopped down. Her elbow eked out a tiny open spot on the table, and she rested her face in one hand. Stuff waiting to be packed covered every other inch of table space.

"I keep hoping you will tell me 'April Fools'." Her mind raced over her problems. "I want my life back."

"Boy, it's been a long week. One more day." Selah dropped her gym bag on the kitchen floor and her stack of schoolbooks on the table.

"Is it going better with Vanessa?" Mom asked.

"She's not said anything to me all week. If I try to talk to her, she says, 'humph' and walks off."

Mom peeled the plastic wrap off a plate of cookies and offered them to Selah. "Girls this age are complicated."

Selah reached for a cookie. "Can I stay with Grandpa next Monday? There's no school."

"That won't work. Actually, Grandpa called today to say Katie's sister has been ill. He said to tell you he's sorry, but he has to take Katie to visit her sister this weekend. He's turning Dream out to pasture, leaving food in the barn for Pearl, and taking Skunk with them. I'm afraid you won't be going to the farm at all." Mom bit into a cookie and tucked a dangling chocolate hunk into her mouth. "You're going to Austin with us to look for a place to live."

Selah's cookie started to taste like lima beans. "Great. Just great." She groaned.

"Selah, please. This isn't easy for any of us. Please be part of the solution. But if you can't change it, take your attitude to your room."

Turbulence raged in Selah's room. She slammed her books on the desk and kicked a defenseless pair of jeans under the bed. "A long weekend wasted."

"Can we ride the jet skis?" Davy's face smashed into the window in the back seat as they drove into Austin.

"Not this trip." Dad pointed out the cliffs lining the Colorado River. "There are hiking trails all over those hills with spectacular views. Once we get settled in here, we will explore them."

Mom flipped through a tourist flyer. "A friend from church told me Austin is full of eateries with major character."

Dad braked for the red light. "Everyone I have told about our moving here says 'we will love it'." He slammed on the brakes as a car squeezed in. "Except for the traffic."

"I'm not going to love it here! Doesn't that matter to anybody?" Selah blurted. "I'm going to start high school. That's a really big deal. I won't know a single person. Everyone will already have their group of friends, and I'll get to be the one they make fun of."

"Are you done, honey? It matters a great deal. We will help you get through it." Mom pointed to the road. "Your turn is coming up," she said to Dad. "The Realtor told me this neighborhood is exactly what we described for our new home. The second road to the left takes us to the recreation center, and she's going to meet us there."

Michael and Davy screeched and bounced in their seats at the sight of water slides along the pool's edge. "Look, Selah. We'll have so much fun there."

"I think it's a hit." Mom laughed at their delight.

"I don't matter in this family," Selah moaned.

Barely able to keep her eyes open to do her homework, Selah rested her face in one hand and tapped her desk with a pencil in the other hand. Wednesdays were always her worst days. Two more days till Friday when Grandpa would come to take her to the farm. She still had to survive the math quiz on Thursday.

The aroma of frying chicken goodness drifted up the stairs to her room and made it even harder to concentrate. Mashed potatoes and gravy would taste good right about now. Mom loved to cook, and Selah loved to eat.

Mom called up the stairs. "Selah, Grandpa's on the phone for you."

Selah jolted alert, raced down, and took the phone from Mom. "Grandpa?"

"Hey, sunshine. How's your shoulder?"

"All better. Not even sore."

"Must be nice to be thirteen and able to bounce back so quickly after a fall. What do you think of the house in Austin?"

"I'm told it's 'perfect'."

"Once you get settled in and find a new friend, you'll like it. Say, I talked to Cooper, and he had another advertiser contact him. They want to give you and Sweet Dream a new aluminum, slant-load horse trailer."

"NO!"

"They want you to go to the website and pick out the design you'd like, and they want to know what color you want the lettering."

"No way!"

"They hope to have it ready to present to you at the Texas Trainers Demonstration Event. It's in Houston in a few weeks. It's a gift, but understand, they're going to want you to represent their products in their advertisements."

"PINK! Make the letters pink."

"You know, I knew you'd say that." Grandpa chuckled. "See you on Friday."

"I can't wait. You're really going to come get me this time?"

"That's the plan. Gotta run, sunshine."

"Will I be able to go to events? Will I get to use a horse trailer?" When Grandpa didn't answer, she realized he'd already hung up.

CHAPTER EIGHT

Selah elbowed the farm kitchen screen door open balancing her orange juice and bag of donuts. She set the glass on the table between the two porch chairs and dipped into the bag.

"If your mother knew you had donuts for breakfast every Saturday morning, she would put a stop to it."

"It's our special secret. Awh. These are still warm."

Grandpa folded the morning paper into his lap. "So, I've not heard much about Austin from you."

"What's to tell? I hate it. It's too far from here."

"There're some really nice areas for horseback riding. Bastrop, for one."

An old truck rattled down the driveway way too fast, blaring the horn. A dust cloud billowed from the road. Grandpa rose from his chair. The tan Ford skidded on the gravel as it stopped. Mr. Noah, from a neighboring farm, leapt out and strode to the deck.

"Chief's been trying to call you, Ed."

Grandpa grumbled at his cell phone as he tapped the ringer on and moaned at the missed calls. "Why didn't he call the house phone?"

Mr. Norris shrugged. "He said you never answer it either. The Bartons have an emergency. Ellie's disappeared."

"Oh no." Grandpa threw the newspaper into the chair behind him.

"One minute she was in the yard playing with her puppy, and the next she was gone. Deputy Bob's called out the search and rescue team. She's been missing for almost three hours now."

Selah's heart sank. "Ellie is only four. She's helpless out there."

Grandpa pulled his Search & Rescue backpack from the closet and crammed his feet into his snake boots. "Have they checked the neighboring farms?"

"The teams on site are combing the area around the Bartons for tracks and scanning with thermal imaging for any sign of her. Chief is already at the scene. He's calling in all the resources this county has, including the bloodhounds from the prison." Mr. Noah fidgeted with the coins in his pocket. "I called Katie, and she will meet us at the Bartons."

"Wise move." Grandpa tucked a water bottle into his pack. "She really knows The Grasslands well. If anybody can find Ellie, it will be Katie." He threw his pack over his shoulder and strode to the truck, calling instructions to Selah. "Stay by the house. Do the rest of the morning chores because I won't be back until we find her."

"But, Grandpa." She raced after him and tugged on his sleeve. "I could help."

He drew her into a hug. "I appreciate your heart, but a search is no place for you. We hope for the best, but we never know what we're going to find." He kissed the top of her head as he released her. "Practice your liberty work with Dream."

Dazed and worried, Selah sleepwalked through the barn chores routine. *Little Ellie.* She ran her hand around Sweet Dream's water bucket, dumped it out, and cranked on the water nozzle to refill it. Dream held her head over the fence rail as she paced the fence line, wearing a path in the grass. "Why are you doing that? What is bothering you?"

Skunk got up and moved to a different spot in the yard for the fourth time. Her nose followed her tail a couple turns around before she settled down again. "You're agitated about something, too."

Selah snatched the halter from the hook. "I'm going to get in trouble for this, but if we find Ellie, he'll forgive me and be so proud of me. I can't just do nothing." Halter over her shoulder, she marched to her horse. "Grandpa will see how much he needs me here." She slapped the pad and saddle on Dream without even brushing her back. "Nobody knows The Grasslands like us, especially not Katie."

She headed out of the farmyard with Dream in an energetic trot. Skunk followed along like the tail of a kite.

They popped out of a forested area and paused, overlooking a meadow. She kicked her feet out of her stirrups, tucked them underneath her, and stood in the saddle still holding the reins. "Which way? So many places to look."

In the distance, a pair of dirt bikes crisscrossed the meadow. When Dream's head flew up watching them, Selah dropped back down into the saddle.

"Easy, girl." She directed the mare down a grassy lane away from the bikes. The horse looked over her shoulder nervously but got back to work.

"Ellie! Where are you?" She listened, hoping to hear a small voice, but then directed Dream north toward the Bartons' farm again. They zigzagged across a wide field searching for any sign. Satisfying herself she'd covered the whole section of grass, she walked along the forest's edge. Peering into the darkness of the deep woods, she scanned for anything out of place. "Ellie!"

After another hour and another meadow thoroughly searched, Selah moved into the shade. *I don't remember turning off the water in the barn.*

Sweet Dream glistened with sweat. Skunk's tongue hung out as she panted. When the sweat pooled in Selah's eyes, she rubbed away the burning salt with her pink T-shirt. "I should have brought some water. Next emergency, I'll remember water." Closer to the Bartons' farm than Grandpa's, Selah decided they better get to water. "I don't want you to have a tummy ache and colic." She patted Dream's sweaty neck.

The closer they got to the Bartons' the more activity they had to navigate. Four-wheelers' and dirt bikes' motors agitated Dream, and Selah had to keep reassuring the mare with a soft voice and one hand rubbing under her mane. "You just don't trust dirt bikes. I won't let them eat you."

The search command-center vehicles overwhelmed the Bartons' driveway. Selah dismounted and led Dream the rest of the way in. Everyone bustled with serious purpose. From the task-focused atmosphere, she didn't need to ask if Ellie had been found.

Dream jumped as the door to the command mobile unit flew open and the chief's head popped out. "They found her!"

Jubilation combined with tears broke out. Standing with a friend, under a shade tree in the yard, Ellie's mother crumpled to the ground in a dead faint. Team members rushed to her side. They soon revived her, gave her water, and helped her to her feet.

Everyone crowded around her. "Great news."

"So grateful."

"Who found her?" someone asked.

"Katie on the Red Team," a command team aide answered.

"Oh, I so knew it. If anyone could find the child, it would be Katie. It's like she gets special instructions from heaven."

"Where was she?"

"The team captain said she was only a half mile from her house, but she was so scared she hid. When she heard *Katie* calling her name, she peeked out of the thicket and answered her."

"Oh, that Katie has a gift."

The group helped Mrs. Barton back to the house, chatting with excitement all the way.

Relief battled disappointment in Selah's heart. She fussed as she walked the mare to a water trough. "It should have been us that found her, Dream."

The teams gathered in the yard and on the porch to watch for the four-wheeler carrying Ellie. Someone shouted, "Here they come."

Others echoed the news.

Ellie's mother went running toward the rescue team, tears streaming down her face. Katie glowed with joy as she stepped off the four-wheeler with Ellie clinging to her. The child's tattered shirt dropped off one shoulder. Dried brown mud covered one foot where a shoe and sock should have been. Ellie's dad rushed past her mom and drew the child from Katie's arms.

Why couldn't it have been anybody but Katie? *Why couldn't I have found her?*

Wrapping his arms around Ellie, her dad held the child like he would never let go of her again. Her mom squeezed in, and for a long moment, the family stood in a tight huddle.

The news crew crowded around with microphones. Mr. Barton paused, turned to them, and spoke to the gathered crowd of reporters, volunteers, well-wishers, and search teams. "How can I ever thank you all enough?" He wiped a tear with his knuckle and smiled as Ellie wrapped herself around her mother and buried her small face under her mother's chin. "The most precious thing in the world has been returned to us because of your efforts. We give all praise, honor, and glory to our Lord Most High." He put his arm around Mrs. Barton and ushered his restored family to the house.

Everyone smiled and hugged Katie. "Congratulations!"

"Well done."

"Great job!"

"It took a team effort," Katie reminded them. "We all had our part to do."

As the reporters began to gather around Katie, the chief strode to her side.

"Chief's running for reelection. He needs all good press he can get," Grandpa said from behind Selah. "Didn't I tell you to stay at the farm?"

"Um...hi, Gr–randpa," she stammered. "I had to come. I love Ellie. I've babysat for her since she was born almost. How could I hang around the farm like it was just a regular day? How could I not do everything I could to help? That was too much to ask of me."

"It wasn't safe for you to be out there on a horse, without a partner, when the helicopters were buzzing the area and search vehicles screaming all over. This is what I mean when I say I'm not up to having you full time." He wagged his finger at her. "You do whatever you want instead of what you've been told to do." He huffed. "Look. I'm exhausted. We'll talk about this later."

Katie stepped toward them with a gay lightness and tucked her hand into the crook of Grandpa's arm. She smiled at Selah and leaned on his shoulder as he drew her away.

Selah tried to smile back. But her heart gave up, and her face sagged.

Grandpa opened the flower-decal-covered passenger side door of Katie's car and gestured grandly for her to slide in. When he shut her door, he moved like a tired man around to the driver side, but his face smiled and he spun his keys around a finger.

"I blew it, Dream, and this is way worse than I thought."

Selah trotted Dream down the driveway. As she rode toward the barn, Grandpa stood outside with his hands tucked in his pockets and his head bowed before the barn. *Is he praying?* Then she cringed. Puddles and streams of water snaked through the barn. Water stood a couple inches deep in Sweet Dream's stall and overflowed in every direction. The bedding washed into the middle of the barn, and the stall could be a wrestling mud pit. Water wicked up through the bales of hay stacked in the adjoining stall. Several water-streaked and discolored bags of fertilizer had shifted and slumped against the wall.

Pearl stalked the top of the stall boards meowing like a wildcat.

Grandpa pivoted to face Selah. "You were told to stay here."

"I'm sorry. I was trying to help." She slid from the saddle.

"Every bit of this is ruined, and I expect you to clean it up." He pointed to the mess. "If Laura wasn't already scheduled to be here tomorrow, I'd take you home this minute. I'll save your lecture on obedience for when I've cooled down." He strode to the house, leaving her in shock.

CHAPTER NINE

Early the next morning, Grandpa's knock rattled Selah's door. "The sun's been up for a while. Laura and Harmony will be here soon."

Selah sprang from bed. "Dream is going to see her mom today." She slipped on a pink T-shirt embroidered with a horse performing a piaffe.

Tugging on her jeans, Selah peered around the door, watching his face. "Are you going to be okay with Miss Laura bringing Grandma's horse here today?"

"I won't lie. It was a gut-wrenching decision. I never wanted to see that horse again in my lifetime." Grandpa turned, and his heavy feet tromped back to the kitchen.

"Ouch. Poor Grandpa." *He'll do anything for me. Even if it hurts.*

As Selah bounced down the stairs after him, he slid the morning paper across the counter. "Great picture of Katie on the front page."

She glanced at Katie's glowing face. "I'm sorry that Harmony coming is so hard. I'm sorry about forgetting to turn the water off. And I'm super sorry about leaving the farm when you told me not to." Selah hugged him around the waist. "I'm new at being a teenager. Please don't be mad at me." She tossed him a charming grin, and he bear-hugged her.

Please love me, Grandpa. Please love me more than Katie.

Dream's head shot up, and blades of grass dribbled from her mouth. The mare stretched tall and focused intently on a rig weaving around the worst of the driveway ruts. The graphics on the side of the two-horse aluminum trailer matched the truck's classy pearl green. Sweet Dream trumpeted a call as she powerwalked the fence line.

"Harmony's here, Grandpa!" a jubilant Selah yelled as if he might miss the commotion.

Grandpa hurried to the truck and opened the door for Laura. When she slid out, she wrapped her arms around him in a long hug. Laura stepped back, holding both of his hands, smiled up at him, and then hugged him again.

Feeling suddenly underdressed, Selah tucked her T-shirt into her jeans as she assessed Laura. She could have stepped into a show ring in her tan jodhpurs and pressed white blouse.

She is really pretty for being so old. As Selah watched, the seed of an idea sprouted in her imagination.

With her arm around his waist and his arm across her shoulder, Laura rotated to Selah. "Oh my, Ed, she looks so much like Mary."

"It's a sweet comfort. Brings a smile to my soul that Selah can't bring herself to wear matching socks."

Laura threw her head back and laughed. "When we were girls, Mary and I always seemed to be in competition about who could wear the most outrageous color combination." Laura's mouth puckered. "I still think about her every day when I choose my socks. I so miss her in my life."

Grandpa studied the toes of his boots.

Dream screamed the loudest whinny Selah had ever heard. The horse in the trailer kicked the door.

"Guess we better reunite mother and daughter before Harmony reduces my trailer to aluminum shavings." As Laura backed the tall, elegant mare from the trailer, Sweet Dream cantered in circles, flipping her nose. The mare shook her head and whinnied loud enough to wake the neighbors. The new arrival whipped her head around to see Dream and answered the call with an urgency of her own. Harmony dragged Laura to the edge of Dream's pasture. The two mares snorted, puffed, and squealed at each other for many long moments.

"They remember!" Laura said. "What a sweet thing."

"Thanks so much for bringing her, Miss Laura. Dream knows her mother!" Selah cried. "I've seen the old video of Grandma riding Harmony, but seeing her for real... Wow. She is gorgeous."

"She has an air about her. She was a striking presence in the show ring. You couldn't help but watch when she performed. She has the grace of a ballerina and the power of a boxer."

"Grandpa, don't you think they have the same expression?" Selah turned to him, but he was disappearing into the house. "Grandpa?"

Blessed with a perfect day, the riders drifted along The Grasslands trail. The sun gently warmed their faces and coaxed sweet oils from the wildflowers to scent the air. The horses crowded together, and Selah's knee bumped into Miss Laura's. But neither had the heart to separate the mares.

"Thanks for sending the flysheet for Dream. She sniffed and snorted at it. I was afraid she would rip it to shreds if I put it on her. It's hanging in the barn where she can see it." Selah stood in one stirrup, brought her saddle back to the center, and did a quick check of her girth. "I loved the picture. It's hard to imagine grandparents when they were young. Grandma was beautiful."

"Yes, she was. Inside and out."

"There was a real pretty girl standing next to Grandpa in the picture."

Laura stifled her laugh and coughed instead. "He was quite the charmer back then. Her name was Fran. She was out of the picture as soon as he saw Mary."

"I knew it! I met her. She's working at the bakery."

"I'm sorry to hear she's turned up in your grandpa's life again. Unless she's changed over the years, she is not good news. He deserves better."

"Agh." Selah slouched in the saddle. "I was counting on her."

"What?"

Oops. Selah stiffened when she realized her error. "Oh, sorry. Sometimes what I'm thinking slips out of my mouth and doesn't make any sense." She diverted to another topic. "Would you tell me what my Grandma Mary was like?"

"Is it still too difficult for your grandfather to talk about, Selah?"

"He changes the subject when I ask about her."

"I understand. Losing her was devastating." Laura focused on her hands on the reins. After a deep breath, she continued, "We were something together. I grew up on my family's Morgan Horse breeding farm. She moved in next door. When she was your age, Mary couldn't even walk. Her papa would carry her out where she could sketch our mares and foals. She fell in love with a foal that had a clubfoot—Illusion. Our barn manager decided to put the filly down, but he was no match for your grandma."

Harmony caught Skunk out of the corner of her eye and skittered sideways a few steps before settling down pressed against Dream. "She had a huge library of horse books and was willing to sell every one of them to raise money for Illusion's surgery. 'Course, she didn't own the filly, and the vet said it didn't have a good chance of fixing the problem. Didn't stop her."

"But she raised the money."

"She did. She was an amazing artist, and we sold stacks of foal sketches at a local fair." Laura half-halted Harmony and pointed out a red-tailed hawk. "We both had a driving passion for horses that cemented us together."

"And you had the idea of the therapeutic riding."

"I'd heard of a disabled woman who won silver in Olympic dressage. I was so inspired—I asked the gardener to help me put straps on a saddle so Mary could ride. The challenge was getting *in* the saddle." Laura smiled and gently shook her head as sweet memories drifted across her face. "We were making progress, too, until the buggy wheel broke as I was taking her home and we got found out."

"Oh."

"Her papa was furious. But by then, she could stand for a few seconds, and she won him over to the point he worked a deal for Illusion with my father. Her papa would do anything for her. We all would. Anyway, they did the surgery and took the foal to Destin for the same aquatic therapy that helped Mary."

"Wow." Selah caressed the sides of Sweet Dream's neck with long, smooth strokes. "It's sad. I barely remember my grandma."

"She always ran her hands down Illusion's and Harmony's neck like you just did." Laura's voice tapered off. "She was the kindest person I ever knew. She had such an easy way about her, not just with horses, but with people, too. When you engaged her in conversation, you got all of her. Her eyes went to yours, and she totally listened to what you were saying. It was like drawing her deep into your soul." Laura sighed and paused. "You never forget someone like her."

The heads of both horses popped up in unison as a coyote slunk across the path. They watched it intently until it disappeared in the underbrush.

"I remember when you were born. Your grandma was so in love. She would chatter on about how she hoped you loved horses. How she wanted to teach you to read and to draw horses and to ride. When you were barely able to sit up, she had you in her lap reading horse stories."

"I think she had every horse book ever written. Grandpa gave her collection to me. They stay here at the farm in her library."

"Sweet. What a wonderful legacy." Laura turned Harmony to the side of the trail and cued her to put her head down so she could snatch the grass. "I like to spoil her." Laura's smile reflected her delight. "I knew the most important thing to your grandma was to give you a horse from Illusion's bloodline. I figured if the foal turned out to be a little horror, I would keep trying until I got the right horse for you." Laura's voice faded. "She would have ultimately done the same thing. Then she would've handled the foal with Harmony's temperamental issues in mind and hoped to overcome them with kindness from the beginning."

"Is that what you did with Dream?"

Laura chuckled. "Dream was my favorite of all my foals that year. She was born a bit early and was fragile for several weeks. She grew into an adorable troublemaker." Her smile broadened. "She always had her nose where it shouldn't be. If there was a bucket knocked off, the teeth marks were hers. If the water-trough float stopped working, it was because she tormented it."

"She's a stinker. Do you know she can pick locks?"

"So many talents."

"Did Grandpa tell you Dream went crazy when a buzzard swooped over us?"

"He mentioned that. But when you first found Dream tangled in the wire, she was surrounded by buzzards. I think she deserves a break on that one." Laura half-halted Harmony again then relaxed the reins. "Horses have great memories. You wish they would forget things that scare them, but that's how they survive in the wild."

Selah leaned forward and threw her arms around Dream's neck. "That explains a lot."

Laura laughed. "I wanted her started right, and I knew Cooper would bring out the best in her. Dream was on her way to Cooper's when the wreck happened and I lost her."

A lightbulb flickered on in Selah's head, and her seed of an idea flowered. *Miss Laura would be better for Grandpa than Miss Katie—and for me, too. She loves to ride, and from the hug she gave Grandpa, she obviously loves him. Miss Laura would want me at the farm to ride with her. This plan could work!* "I'm glad you came today. Grandpa has been very lonely, and I could tell he was really happy to see you."

"Your grandpa is a dear man."

She does like him! "I would like to learn dressage. Do you think you could come to the farm more often? Dream would like it, too."

"That would bless your grandma's heart. Actually, I've meant to come long before now and was about to suggest it." Laura's words poured out in a rush. "It does look like Dream has the ability. She's got a nice cadence to her step, and you could easily teach her collection and dressage movements. I would love to help."

"That would be amazing!" Selah squealed. "I want to do a piaffe in the worst way." *If she likes him and he likes her and they both like me, I'll be moving to the farm.*

When Selah and Laura returned to the farm, they rode into the arena.

"Your lateral flexibility is excellent, Selah. Dream is sensitive and soft on the bit."

"Mr. Cooper taught her."

"The next step is to add a little leg pressure and make contact with her mouth. When you feel her relax and give into your hands—give back to her immediately. She learns from the release of pressure."

Selah picked up the reins and made light contact with the bit. Sweet Dream backed up.

"Watch Harmony. Use a little momentum to teach this at first." Laura demonstrated. "Once you have her responding nicely to your hands, you can get movements like this from her." Laura gathered Harmony and moved forward in an energetic prance.

"Ahhh... Yes, I want that!" Selah tried again.

"Her back will round up, and you will begin to feel a floating lightness in her movements."

Grandpa strode to the arena fence. As he propped one boot on the bottom rail, he waved and hollered, "How did the ride go?"

"Good. No, great!"

"Delightful," added Laura. "We had a wonderful time."

"You two gonna ride all day?"

"What a great idea, Grandpa. Miss Laura is showing me how to teach Dream some collection. And she promises to come back soon and give me dressage lessons." On impulse, Selah asked, "Miss Laura, could I ride Harmony?"

Laura appeared stricken as she glanced at Grandpa.

Grandpa's face turned white as stone, and fury colored his voice. "No!" He whipped around and walked back to the house.

Tears blurred Selah's eyes. "Grandpa's never talked to me like that."

"Selah, even though the vet has her on calming supplements, Harmony is unpredictable. That's sometimes the hallmark of a horse with extreme talent. Your grandpa is right."

"Was Harmony dangerous for my grandma? Is that what's bothering Grandpa?"

"Has no one ever told you how your grandmother died?"

"No, ma'am. They only say it was a horse accident."

"No wonder, really. It's been extremely painful for the whole family. I try to focus on the good memories, but the pain of her loss overpowers them." Laura dismounted and walked Harmony to the gate.

"Even though Harmony was breathtakingly beautiful in the dressage ring, she could erupt in an unexplainable tantrum in an instant. That kind of crazy didn't come from Illusion's bloodline. Harmony was especially anxious, so your grandma was riding her on the outskirts of the show grounds to get away from the energy of the show. A young kid on a motorbike blasted up a side trail and skidded out in front of her. Harmony reared, twisted in the air, and lost her footing. They fell over backward down an embankment."

"Poor Grandpa." Selah bit her lip and noticed she was holding her breath.

"It was horrific. If only..." Laura sighed. "The show closed immediately. The club rallied around and held vigil at the hospital. Prayer warriors from the church filled the hospital hallway." She rested her hand on Harmony's neck. "Mary was in ICU for several days, but she never regained consciousness."

Selah slid from her saddle.

Laura gazed into the pasture, heaved an exhale, and returned her focus to Selah. "You were her sun and moon and stars. She was in a coma so I don't know if your grandma could hear me, but I promised her I would raise a foal for you and teach you what she would have taught you." She hugged Selah. "She would have done the same for me."

"Poor Grandpa," Selah repeated as she pushed open the gate and held it for Laura. They walked without speaking toward the barn.

Laura stopped by her trailer. Harmony lowered her head so Laura could unbuckle the bridle. "After the accident, Harmony had to be heavily sedated to load her in the trailer and get her to the vet hospital. After several weeks there, Harmony came home with me." She loosened Harmony's girth and pulled the saddle from her back. "She was a changed horse. Her spirit was broken. Her eyes were dull and listless. She will do what I ask of her, but she lacks her former brilliance of movement." A faraway look glazed Laura's eyes. "Taking Harmony was the least I could do for Mary. She was more than my best friend. She was like part of who I am. It's even worse for your grandpa." Laura slipped her saddle into the tack compartment.

"So then Grandpa got rid of all the horses?" Dream searched Selah's back pockets for a treat. "Do you know where Grandpa's paint gelding went?"

"He walked away from what he'd loved all his life. For him to sell Buddy shows you how shattered his heart was. I have no idea what happened to his paint horse." Laura closed and secured the tack compartment door. "Raising a horse for you helped me heal."

"I'm glad you took Harmony. Otherwise, I wouldn't have Dream. She's my heart-horse. Her ending up lost in The Grasslands and me finding her feels like something angels worked out."

"Maybe an angel named Mary. It does feel like a miracle, doesn't it?" Harmony loaded into the trailer and whinnied to Dream. "It would make her smile to know you're riding a mare from the bloodline of *her* heart-horse. Think of it—a great-great-granddaughter of Illusion. Yes, she's smiling."

"I want to ride just like my grandma." Selah pulled off her helmet. "Wish this day didn't have to end."

Now to hint to Grandpa that Miss Laura likes him. If this works right, I'll not be moving to Austin. No way, nohow!

As Selah popped into the kitchen, her enthusiasm bubbled from her mouth. "Isn't this an amazing day?"

"That's one way to characterize it." Grandpa slipped his wallet into his back pocket and snatched his keys from the rack. He headed out the door. "Put a spin on it because I need to get you home."

She grabbed up her things stacked by the door and chased after him. "Are you mad at me again? I said I was sorry about leaving the water on. Is it about Harmony? I'm sorry I didn't think."

"You have a way of getting under my skin."

She tossed her pack in the back seat and hopped in. "I'm real sorry."

He started the truck. "I get it and you're forgiven."

"So why are you taking me home early?"

"There's a program at Katie's church tonight. She wants me to go along."

Selah tugged on the threads of a small hole in her jeans. "Have you ever thought about asking Miss Laura to go out on a date?"

Grandpa groaned and looked over at her. He rolled his eyes and turned back to the road. "No, and I will arrange my own life—thank you very much."

"But she's great, and you have so much in common."

"We have a deep wound of the heart in common."

"But, Grandpa, I could tell she likes you."

"Selah, you call her 'Miss' Laura because that is how your mom taught you to address adults, but Laura is married."

Selah choked on her disappointment. "No."

"Anyway, movin' on. The plan for next weekend is to get you to the stadium in Houston by nine a.m. Cooper is sending the van to pick up Dream on Friday so all the horses can settle in overnight. There will be time for you to rehearse with Jordan before the demo."

"I'm really nervous about riding in front of those people. I haven't had near enough time with Dream. I should be staying."

"And miss school? I don't think so. Believe it or not, your schoolwork is more important than your riding."

"I don't have a life unless I'm with Dream."

CHAPTER TEN

The next weekend, Selah led Sweet Dream down a narrow alley to the arena to meet Jordan. A girl with long brown hair, dressed in jodhpurs and tall black boots stood with her back to Selah, blocking the way.

"Vanessa?"

The girl flipped around, and surprise widened her eyes. "Selah."

"What're you doing here?" Selah drew closer to Sweet Dream.

"My trainer brought a horse to the demonstration event for me. It's a massive Friesian."

"What about the Warmblood from Germany?"

"She didn't turn out to be a good fit."

"I'm so sorry. I know you had your heart set on her working out."

"She had some bone splints and seemed a little off. The vet recommended we pass on her. The trainer thinks we can do a lot better. Daddy wants the best."

"I have to do a freestyle demo in a few minutes. Why don't you come cheer us on?"

Vanessa fluffed her bangs. "Can't. Have to run." She turned on her fancy black boot heel and waltzed away, tapping her crop lightly at the top of her tall boot.

Selah felt like a bread crumb dropped on the floor. "Was she really ever my best friend?"

Jordan trotted her colt down the rail. "Where have you been? We don't have much practice time in the arena before everything starts. Follow me, and I'll show you exactly what we're going to demo today."

"Sorry, Jordan. I saw a girl who used to be my best friend, only she's not."

"That's a tough one. Sorry about your friend." Jordan reined the little gelding to a stop. "You know these trail exercises so just go through the drill with me." Jordan trotted her horse with Selah following closely.

"If you don't have any friends, they can't rip your heart out." Selah pivoted Dream and cantered after Jordan. After a couple practice turns, the pairs stood together and rested. "Since I'm moving to Austin, I'll never see her again. Sure does hurt though when I think about what she said about me." Selah stroked her mare's neck. "That's not really even the worst of it. I'm trying to convince Grandpa I should come live with him, but he won't listen." She flopped forward and wrapped both arms around the horse's neck. "All he can think about is Katie.

Katie this and Katie that. Stuff blasts out of my mouth about Katie that makes Grandpa upset at me. I don't even mean to, but I can't help it."

"Sounds like the frustrations of being a teenager. It's all part of growing up. The best advice I can give you is to always be kind. Bless others and you will be blessed."

"You're scaring me."

"Why?"

"You sound like my mother."

Grandpa and Katie hurried toward Selah as she waited outside the gate with the horses. Katie extended a necklace to Selah with both hands. "I want you to have this. It's an essential oils diffuser. It even has a horse on it." Katie's eyes asked Selah to take it. "I've already put peppermint in there to help keep your stomach settled. I know how queasy you get when you get nervous."

The longer Katie stood with her hands up offering Selah the gift, the more awkward it got. With a quick glance at Grandpa, she took and pocketed the silver necklace.

"Aren't you going to wear it?" Grandpa asked. "It was very nice of Katie to get that for you."

"It was nice of you, thank you, Katie," Selah said dutifully. "But we are performing a spin, and it might knock my teeth out."

Grandpa frowned at Selah, put his arm around Katie, and ushered her away to find seats to watch the demonstration.

"Arg. I can't do anything right." Selah closed her eyes and leaned her head on Dream.

SUSAN COUNT

Jordan hustled toward them as she adjusted the mouthpiece on her headset. "Check," she said to the media booth. "Okay, Selah, mount up. We're on."

They rode, side by side, into the center of the arena to light applause.

Selah waved. *I'm already glad I skipped breakfast. I feel like puke. Maybe a whiff of the peppermint would have been a good idea.*

Jordan glanced at Selah like she knew what Selah was thinking.

"Good morning." Jordan waved to the audience. "I'm Jordan, and this colt is Rain Man. He is a two-year-old, and he's had about ninety days of training. Selah is riding Sweet Dream, who is a graduate of the Cooper Start 'Em Right Program." Jordan pivoted the horse on his haunches to engage all of the audience. "We'd like to show you a couple of routines we use to teach them to be safe and respectful trail horses." She eased Rain Man into a walk on a loose rein.

"We get calls for help with horses that jig or won't walk on the trail. We are going to demo a quick exercise you can use to teach your students how to deal with it. If you'd like more ideas, Mr. Cooper has an in-depth DVD for sale at our booth."

Selah tasted a little bile as she lined Dream up behind Jordan.

"For this exercise, your student needs a partner to train with. Trot the horses down the trail, have them take turns making the call to change directions. At the call, stop, roll back, and trot on. Don't go very far, twenty-five feet or so. After a few of those exercises, give them the opportunity to walk quietly away from the barn. As long as they're relaxed, reward them by letting them walk. If they jig, repeat the exercise."

Jordan reined the colt to a stop and continued to teach. "We get requests for help with horses wanting to bolt back to the barn. If a horse is barn sour, make the barn a place of work. Put some energy into the horse's feet and do circles, figure eights, and serpentines."

Selah focused on the movements she was demonstrating rather than her clenched stomach as Jordan explained them to the crowd.

"Ride on out again, and if the horse wants to go back to the barn—no worries!—put its feet to work. Repeat as often as necessary. We want to make the right thing easy for the horse." Jordan stopped in the center and cued Rain Man into a slow-stepping spin. "Thank you all for coming. We enjoyed showing you our trail exercises. Stop by and see us at our booth." Jordan and Selah separated and side-passed down the fence rails, waving goodbye to the crowd.

The knot in Selah stomach loosened. *I made it without barfing, but barely. I wonder if the oil would help?*

"Selah." Cooper's deep voice boomed over the sound system. "Come back into the arena, please."

She spun Dream, and they cantered to the center of the arena.

"Folks, I want you to keep a close eye on Selah over the next few years. She's already demonstrated an understanding of horses way beyond her years. She is only twelve and—"

Selah threw her hand in the air with three fingers raised.

"Excuse me, thirteen. The team on my ranch loves her and is excited to be the ones who have helped get her started and launch her career."

She looked down at the saddle horn and wished Mr. Cooper would stop gushing over her.

"Selah, we have a little something for you. Close your eyes." She put one hand over her eyes but spread her fingers wide.

"You're peeking."

She nodded yes as she clamped her other hand over the first and squeezed her fingers together.

A wide gate at the far end of the arena swung open. A truck, pulling a horse trailer, rumbled into the arena and made a lap around the rail before stopping behind her.

"Keep your eyes closed," Cooper warned. "Ladies and gentlemen, in cooperation with Murphy Trailers, I'm happy to announce the sponsorship of a pair of rising stars in youth equestrian events, Selah and Sweet Dream!"

Selah couldn't keep her eyes closed any longer.

"Did I say you could open your eyes?" Cooper challenged.

Selah laughed and shook her head no.

"Maybe you should look behind you."

She twisted in the saddle and gasped. "Wow!" She urged Dream into a canter, and they circled the shiny rig.

"Check out Selah and Sweet Dream on her new blog," Cooper told the crowd.

She rode to the side of the silver trailer and touched the pink lettering of Sweet Dream's name. As her finger traced the letter S, Vanessa snapped their picture and posted it on her Facelook page with the caption—"Ha-ha. Selah's in kindergarten trying to learn how to write the letter S."

The driver of the dually got out of the truck and opened the door to the horse compartment.

Cooper challenged her. "Load her up, Selah. See if it suits her."

Selah cued the mare to canter on the rail, making one lap around. They gathered speed heading to the trailer door. A few strides from the door, the crowd gasped as she collected Dream's stride. Selah kicked her feet out of the stirrups, grabbed the edge of the trailer roof to lift herself from the saddle as Dream disappeared into the compartment. Selah dropped to the ground and waved. With Dream's black head sticking out the window, the driver shut the back door to thunderous applause.

"If you remember, Dream was in a trailer wreck as a two-year-old. What you just witnessed is what you can overcome when you learn to be your horse's leader. But, folks, don't try this at home. Selah's been practicing the steps to this trick under my direct supervision. If you want to know more, come by the booth and talk to us."

"I've signed so many pictures this fancy pen is running out of ink!" Selah shook the pen to coax out another drop.

Jordan examined the necklace around Selah's neck. "That's beautiful. Is it a diffuser?"

"Yup. From Queen Katie. If I want a ride home, I have to wear it. It's supposed to help me not get sick."

"If there is a chance it will help you not throw up, you should wear it. You hold the world record for puking on camera." Jordan restacked flyers on the display table. "I hope we brought enough of your DVDs."

"Dream and I are famous. Look how many people have signed up for my blog."

"Showtime." Jordan untied Dream and handed the lead rope to Selah. "I know you're worried about the liberty work. I've only got you doing the elementary exercises, and Dream can do those perfectly."

"But we've just started doing the exercises without a lead rope."

"What's the worst that can happen?" Jordan lifted both her palms. "She might mess up a little, and you'll have to get her attention back on you."

Selah gestured toward the stands. "Those are expert trainers."

"They don't expect you to be perfect. You're the only one who puts that kind of pressure on you. Besides, it's not like she can get out of the arena. She did great in practice."

"Thanks for your faith in me, Jordan. I have learned so much from you."

"You're ready. Time to get your feet wet. Now breathe the scent from the diffuser."

Waiting for the carriage driving demo team to finish, Selah stood looking into the arena through a crack in the gate. She crushed her face against Dream's neck. "I'm scared, Dream." Sweet Dream turned her head to nuzzle Selah. "Looks like millions of professional trainers out there. Trainers who know what they're doing. And they're watching us."

When Selah's music started, she unconsciously lifted the necklace to her nose. She breathed in the aroma Katie said would help her not puke from nerves. "Let's go dancing, Dream." With Sweet Dream at the end of a long line, Selah sprinted into the arena, asking the horse to circle her. Selah changed direction abruptly, and the mare pivoted to copy her movements.

She removed the halter and lead rope from Dream's head, dropping them near the gate. Now with no rope between them, Selah used the body language and cues she'd taught the horse to guide her around the arena.

Picking up a trot, Dream circled Selah, who dodged and turned as if to lose her shadow. But the mare mirrored Selah's every move. When Selah ran as if cantering, the horse mimicked the steps. Then Dream fell behind her a stride, and Selah lost sight of the horse in her peripheral vision.

"Stay with me, Dream. We're almost done. I'll look silly if you leave me here cantering all by myself in front of all these trainers." But the air around Selah felt too quiet, too empty. Then she heard hooves galloping away and the collective gasp of the audience. As she spun, her mouth opened wide.

Vanessa got and posted her second picture of Selah. This one with the comment, "Can anyone help Selah? She seems to have lost her horse."

Dream barreled down the length of the arena toward a child at the far end. The barefooted boy's hands were raised as he spun chasing a ray of light.

As Dream neared the child, her gait changed to a floating prance with her tail flipped up. She halted and the dust settled. The mare stood with her attention riveted on the small boy. So intent on making his world go around, the child didn't seem to notice the mare. Dream edged forward in slow motion to close the gap between them.

The announcer asked quietly, "Does anyone know this child? Can somebody on the gate crew get to the boy?"

Selah raced to the announcer's box. "I'll get Dream." As fast as she could, without running, Selah hurried toward the horse and the child.

The announcer instructed the audience in hushed tones. "Ladies and gentlemen, please keep your seats and stay very quiet. I'm told the child's mother is on her way from the security booth where she was reporting him lost. Selah will round up Sweet Dream, and we can help by being still."

Dream had stirred the little boy's awareness now and inched closer to him. She moved her soft muzzle to rest it by one of the boy's tiny ears, and the child stilled, smiled, and curled up his shoulder like he was being tickled. His small hand rubbed an equally small circle on her muzzle, and his head tilted way back to look into her eyes. As Dream's mouth touched his cheek, his fingers explored her nostrils and stroked her face. His mouth opened wide. His arms rose up and his hands twirled. Soon, his arms were spinning in a wide arc. His dark eyes shone as his body spun and swayed. The mare inched after him. With his hands on either side of her muzzle, he held his face next to hers.

The child stumbled into the horse's shoulder and fell underneath her. With the child sprawled awkwardly beneath Dream, not a muscle on her body moved. The audience held its breath as the child wrapped itself around the horse's extended front leg in a hug and drew himself up from the ground. The boy rocked from side to side around her leg with his head flung back and a blissful smile on his face.

Selah put one hand on the mare and offered the other hand to the boy. She drew him toward the fence where his mother waited. Dream followed them with her nose stretched toward the child. As his mother gathered him, he pointed to Dream and bounced in his mother's arms. Selah retrieved the boy's shoes and socks, scattered about with reckless abandon. Her heart swelled at the obvious pleasure the child had gotten from playing with Dream.

Selah scanned the arena rail for Grandpa. *Are you watching? Do you see how special Dream is?*

Grandpa made his way to Selah from the far end of the arena. Katie walked beside him, carrying a white paper plate with a huge funnel cake.

"Wasn't Dream amazing, Grandpa?" Dream extended her nose to Selah for her halter.

"Sorry, sunshine. I missed it." He took Katie's arm and motioned for her to sit down. He handed the warm cake to Selah. "The line for funnel cakes was really long, and I didn't keep a good eye on the time."

"You missed it?" Her mouth sagged open in disbelief.

"I'm sure Cooper recorded it. I'm going to check with Jordan and see if they're done with you. Katie's getting tired, and I'd like to take her home." Grandpa looked with concern at Katie now seated on a nearby bleacher.

"You missed it," Selah muttered again.

As Selah opened the arena gate, a woman hurried toward her.

"Oh, Selah. May I have a moment?"

Selah didn't answer such an oddly phrased question but watched the thin, well-dressed lady approach. Her long dark hair tucked to the side with a sparkly gold clip.

"I'm an old friend of Cooper's and a huge fan of yours. I'm Cindy."

"Thank you. Nice to meet you." Selah nodded, turned away to stroke Dream's neck. "Miss Jordan makes me look good. She's over there by the gate. She can help you with any issues you're having with your horse. I'm just a student, really."

"You don't understand. I'm not looking for a trainer. A mutual friend, Amanda, gave me an article from your local paper."

"Oh yeah. We eat lunch together at school."

"Amanda boards her horse at my barn. The ingenuity and courage you showed saving the forest ranger inspired me and touched my heart." Cindy laid her hand over her heart. "All I could think was this should be a movie."

"A real movie about Dream?"

"And just now, watching your horse interact with the little boy? I'm awestruck."

Grandpa raised his voice above the noise of the surrounding bustle. "Selah, run Dream back to her stall and dash to Murphy's Trailer booth. They want to interview you before they leave."

"But?"

"Hurry."

Selah's shoulders slumped. "Excuse me. I gotta go."

"Take my card. We can talk later."

Selah shoved the card in her back pocket without looking at it.

After the interview, Selah hurried back to meet Grandpa. Popping another bite of her funnel cake and savoring the powdered sugar, Selah noticed a horse flash by going way too fast. In the nearby practice arena, a tall, thin woman shrieked, "Sit back in the saddle and pull on the reins."

The rider pulled hard, but the horse's nose stuck in the air and braced against the rider's hands. It took Selah a minute to register the rider was Vanessa.

Selah balanced her funnel cake and ran to the arena. "Vanessa, listen to me," she shouted over the thunder of the horse's hooves as they careened past. "Pull on one rein. Tip his head to the inside. Turn him in a circle." As Selah climbed the fence rails, her cake slipped from the plate and splattered in the dirt. "Keep steady pressure on the inside rein and bump the outside rein."

Vanessa's ponytail flew behind her. Selah cupped one hand around her mouth. "Keep the pressure on. Start making the circle smaller. Keep bumping the outside rein."

Vanessa pulled the horse around enough so it dropped down into a trot and, finally, a walk.

A man's deep voice carried through the whole building. "You should've been able to handle the horse after all the money I've spent on your lessons." Vanessa's father left a plume of cigar smoke behind when he exited.

Vanessa slid from the saddle and handed the reins to the stunned and mute trainer. Tears streaked Vanessa's perfect face as she walked away. Selah followed her for a minute and then ran to catch up. "Vanessa."

"Leave me alone, Selah."

"Vanessa, the horse is a horror, and I'm amazed you stayed on."

"It belongs to an important client of Daddy's. He thinks if he buys the horse, the client will buy the deal. I hate horses."

"You don't mean that. You love riding, and you're amazing at it."

"So good, I had a horse run away with me right in front of some of the best trainers in the state. That's really good, all right. I tried everything I knew to stop the horse and couldn't." She wiped a tear away. "But you knew how to stop it. Why did you help me after I've been so mean to you?"

"You're my friend, Vanessa." Selah hugged her. "You do owe me a funnel cake, though. Listen, I have to get back to the booth. Come with me?"

"Thanks. I wish I could, but my father is waiting. I remember now why you've been my best friend."

Selah flutter-waved goodbye to her friend. "I'll see ya at school."

"Um. I need to talk to you about something." Vanessa bit her upper lip and sucked it into her mouth. "I…"

Grandpa motioned to Selah. "Grandpa's waving like a crazy man for me to come. He's already steamed at me. I gotta go."

That night Selah read through the comments by her classmates on the pictures Vanessa posted. She grabbed for the diffuser necklace, but before she could even breathe in peppermint, she threw up in her desk drawer.

CHAPTER ELEVEN

J’ve never needed spring break like I do now.” At the end of a long week, Selah pushed open the door to the kitchen like it was a boulder. *I can't move to Austin, but I have to get out of that school.*

“Hello.” Mom greeted her. “How was your day?”

“I made it. Kids are still drawing *S*'s in the air. I found another Big Chief tablet stuck to my locker. What got me through was thinking of a whole week at Grandpa's. Is he on his way to pick me up?”

Mom rolled cookie dough in cinnamon and sugar. “Grandpa called.”

Both Selah's hands held her forehead. “Oh no! He's still coming to get me, right?”

“Yes. But a slight delay. We're all going out to eat dinner with Grandpa and Katie Sunday night. You will want to put on something pretty.”

“He always comes to get me on Friday?” Selah pouted. “What's up with that?”

"Not sure yet. It has us curious. Your grandpa was a little mysterious, actually."

This can't be good. Selah's eyes clamped closed. *I can't take anything else, and I hate surprises.* "What am I going to do all day Saturday?"

"Don't worry. I have plenty you can do. The attic needs sorting for one. Perfect job for you."

Selah groaned. "It's my spring break."

Selah grimaced as Davy crammed his mouth with peanuts. He grinned, and a peanut dropped to the table. He was still learning to use his new front teeth. "This is a fun restaurant, Grandpa. I love the peanut shells on the floor."

Grandpa laughed and slid more peanuts toward Davy. "Enjoy yourself."

Both Grandpa and Katie were dressed fancy. Katie wore a dress with a delicate sweater topper embroidered with daisies. Grandpa wore a sport coat over his pearl snap shirt. *Something important is going on.* Selah's toe crunched the shells, but her eyes never left Grandpa while she waited for bad news.

"Thought a fun, Texas tradition would be the perfect setting for some news Katie and I have." Grandpa stood and lifted his glass of red wine. "Family, that I love and hold dear, I have an important announcement that I hope will come as a welcome surprise."

Selah gritted her teeth.

"You know Katie and I have been spending a lot of time together." He looked around the table, smiling. Then his gaze rested on Katie. "We enjoy each other's company and have become best friends. Now I want to make Katie part of our family."

Selah clutched her napkin. Her heart crunched like peanut shells.

Grandpa ignored the pained look on her face. "I have asked Katie if she could love an old geezer, and she says she does. She has swept me off my feet and brought life back to my dry bones."

Katie beamed at him.

"I am honored to tell you she has agreed to become my wife." He clinked his glass with hers. "We are thinking a May wedding."

"So soon," Selah squeaked and immediately covered her mouth, hoping no one heard her over the noise in the restaurant.

Katie thrust her hand into the center of the table showing everyone the engagement ring. Mom burst into tears through a large smile and hugged Katie. Dad stood, shook Grandpa's hand, and clapped him on the back.

"Will you be our new grandma?" Davy asked.

"I would be honored to have you think of me as your grandma, Davy."

Grandpa reached for Katie's hand and drew her to her feet. He pulled her close to him and kissed her with sweet tenderness.

Right here in front of everybody! Selah scowled. *Disgusting.*

The people at tables around them raised their glasses. "Congratulations," echoed through the room.

Selah's face felt frozen. *If I were to smile accidentally right now, my face would crack and fall off. If this isn't a bad dream, then my chances of moving to the farm just went to zip, zilch, zero!*

After dinner, Grandpa shut the truck door for Katie. "How did your week go?" he asked Selah as she climbed into the back seat.

"Fine."

"Vanessa a little easier to get along with since you saved her neck at the demo?"

"Yeah."

"Caroline still coming for a couple days on Monday?"

"Uh-uh."

"Would pizza be good for dinner tomorrow?"

"I guess."

Grandpa and Katie looked at each other, and silence hung over the rest of the trip to the farm.

The next morning, Dr. Steve's truck rumbled into the barnyard, and Selah sprinted outside to greet Caroline.

"Where did you find this?" Selah pinched the hem of Caroline's shirt to straighten the fabric so she could admire it better. "Does it come in pink?"

"I looked in the artist's shop on Deviant Art for a pink one for you, but the site only has wall art. Mom had this put away for my birthday, and she doesn't remember where she got it."

"I love watercolor horses." Selah ooohed.

"The artist's name is Elena Shevd. She is from Russia. I'm saving my money to buy all her horse art. To find her on the site, you have to type her name as one word. I'll show ya later."

The girls chatted with their heads together as Dr. Steve unloaded Caroline's horse. "Think they ever run out of things to say?" he asked Grandpa.

Grandpa took the lead rope from him and put the red sorrel mare into a stall next to Sweet Dream. "Never gonna happen. They're so close, they remind me of Mary and her friend, Laura."

Selah tossed a glance over her shoulder at Grandpa and leaned closer to Caroline's ear. "You couldn't have picked a better time to come," she whispered. "Have you heard about Grandpa and Katie?"

"Just rumors in town about them dating—remember I called you?"

Selah glanced over her shoulder to be sure Grandpa was far enough away not to hear. "It's worse than that. They are getting *marrr–rry–ed*." She drew out every tone.

"Oh, great news." Caroline's eyes brightened.

"What? Great?"

"I'm taking art lessons from Katie. She's really, really nice."

"The next time you take an art lesson you'll be coming here to the farm. She'll be here, and I'll be stuck in Austin."

"No! That's the worst." Caroline grabbed Selah's upper arms. "I'll never see you again."

"I've got to work it out so Grandpa comes up with the plan of me living here. I have an idea, but I need your help."

"Girls, get the mare some hay and water," Grandpa called as he walked the vet back to his truck.

Caroline tossed her duffel bag on the porch. Selah and Caroline raced into the feed room and out again carrying hay.

"Bye, Daddy." Caroline waved as she and Selah scooted past the men again on their way to the house.

Selah took Caroline by the wrist and pulled her into Grandpa's office. "I found a file on the horse I've been looking for. Keep an ear out for Grandpa while I grab it. I want to keep it a surprise for him."

Caroline peered down the hall.

Selah slid out a file drawer, extracted a manila folder, and slipped it under her shirt. "Let's go to my room," she whispered.

Closing the door, she peeked out the window as Grandpa walked into the workshop. "Okay, we're good." She spread papers from the file across her bed. "This file says he gave the horse to a man named Tom Banks." Selah pointed to the notation. "I did a local search but didn't find anything. Do you know him?"

"Tom is Tommy. He's friends with my brother. Tommy joined the Army when my brother left for college."

"Where did he live?"

"With his grandparents somewhere around here."

"Somewhere?"

"I don't know where!" insisted Caroline. "Isn't there anything in the file beside Tommy's name?"

"No."

Caroline froze and pointed to the picture on Selah's wall.

"What's wrong?" Selah asked.

"I think I know that horse."

"You do? His picture has been hanging on my wall forever, and you just now figure out you know him? That's the horse I'm looking for!"

"The markings look the same, but I'm not positive. I go around on farm calls with my dad sometimes, and I think I saw it a few months ago. He was such a sweetheart—I remember him. He kept searching me for treats."

"He used to love peppermints."

"I had a peppermint in my pocket," Caroline said.

"That's him! Was he sick? Is that why your dad was there?"

"No, Dad was looking at a horse lying down with colic. There were about six horses in the pasture. Dad was mumbling about people just turning horses out to pasture and not caring for them."

"Where is he?"

"Old Man Pott's farm."

"I've never heard of him."

"He's a hermit. He lives past Katie's and past the Bartons' and I think one more farm."

"We can get there easy. Let's go." Selah led the way to the barn. The girls were quiet and serious as they tacked up the horses.

Grandpa tossed a hammer into a bucket on his four-wheeler. "Is something up, girls? You're awfully quiet."

"We're going to go ride, Grandpa. Keep Skunk here, okay?"

"Well, I figured that. Come on, Skunk." Grandpa went away muttering.

Selah urged Sweet Dream into an extended trot, and Caroline tried to keep up. "The fast trot on this horse will jar my teeth out," she called.

"You're right. Let's canter."

"Let's race instead," Caroline yelled as she blasted past Dream. The horses' hooves pounded the trail. They stretched out as their strides quickened and their manes whipped the air.

"Yee-ha!" Selah screeched. *I'm comin' to get you, Buddy. I don't know how yet, but you're coming home.*

"Let's go over into the woods so Katie won't see us go by her farm." Selah spoke in a hush as if Katie could hear her.

"You're paranoid. Katie won't think anything, except we're out riding. She won't know we're on a secret mission."

"Well, I don't trust her."

"It sounds like she's going to be your new grandma, so you better get over it. Maybe she's the one you should be working on since you're not getting anywhere with your grandpa."

"I don't know what I'm gonna do. I thought Grandpa might date Miss Laura, only I found out she's married. My family is jazzed about moving to Austin. Mom already has most of the house packed."

"Sounds like you're sunk. I'll miss you."

Selah twisted to look Caroline full in the face. "That's it? You'll miss me."

"You could try being nice to Katie."

"Anything, except that. But I'm not giving up."

"Your grandpa is getting married. He's not going to want you here since you don't like Katie." Caroline shifted in the saddle. "You might as well get used to the idea. You're moving."

"Are you my friend? Or have I mistaken you for someone else?"

"You need to hear the truth, Selah."

"I still have a trick up my sleeve. Starting with this horse of Grandpa's. If Grandpa gets back into horses, it'll keep him too busy for Katie."

"You're hallucinating."

Selah and Caroline crossed the back of the Bartons' farm and stopped at the property line. "Is this Pott's farm?"

"Maybe." Caroline pointed to the overgrown pasture. "I'm pretty sure this is the right farm because it's all weeds and dirt."

"If this isn't Pott's, we'll just go to the next farm."

"He's along here somewhere. Do you think it will be okay to go through the gate?" Caroline asked.

"Sure it is, as long as we shut it." Selah lifted both her shoulders in a question. "What's the worst that could happen?"

"We could get shot at."

"People don't shoot at girls out riding, Caroline."

"Crazy people do, and Old Man Pott's crazy."

"You can wait here if you want. I have to go," Selah declared. "You coming or not?"

"Against my better judgment, but I'm with you."

The girls rode across the weedy pasture toward a rickety barn. Caroline's horse lifted her head high with her ears pricked forward as she pranced sideways.

"You're making her nervous holding her so tight. Ease up on the reins and relax."

"You relax. I'm scared to death."

A dog barked up by the house. Then another and another. Soon, a pack of dogs tore down the hill at them.

"You didn't say anything about assassin dogs."

The dogs surrounded the horses. Caroline's horse reared repeatedly as she held on tight. Sweet Dream flipped her nose and struck at one of the dogs, nailing it in the shoulder. It yelped and slinked off. Another dog streaked around behind Sweet Dream, and one well-placed hind hoof sent it flying. The remaining pack kept their distance, all the while growling and barking.

A shrill whistle blasted, and the dogs ran in the direction of the barn.

"Mr. Pott!" Caroline called. "It's me, Caroline. Dr. Steve's daughter."

He showed himself around the corner of the barn. "What are y'all doing here?" he hollered.

"This is Selah. I told her about your paint horse, and she wants to look at it."

"You lookin' to buy a horse?"

"Maybe, if he's the right one," Selah answered.

"All right. Come on up. I've got horses for sale." Mr. Pott plodded to the feed room and came back with a coffee can of grain. He dumped a few morsels of grain into buckets hanging on the fence and banged on a triangle to call the herd. A couple of the horses almost trotted, but the others walked and limped to the fence.

"These horses are in bad shape," Selah cupped her hand over her mouth and whispered to Caroline. "Look how hard they are trying to get here to eat almost nothing. That poor white mare looks like a bag of bones."

"Shhh… Mr. Pott will hear you. They're way worse than when I came with Dad last fall."

Selah slipped off Dream and handed the reins to Caroline. As she walked to the fence to look closer at the paint horse, her eyes brimmed with tears. Once beautiful, his tail was rubbed raw, his long mane hopelessly knotted, his hooves cracked and split. One white front hoof shone with a massive red bruise on the hoof wall. The swollen knee on the same leg looked the size of a well-watered melon. Thick ooze flowed from his crusted, matted eyes. Black flies swarmed and crawled over raw sores on his hips.

"Those flies lay eggs that hatch into maggots," Caroline whispered over Selah's shoulder. "We have to get him out of here."

Dream nudged Selah from behind as if she agreed.

Selah's hands and jaw muscles knotted. "We have to get all of them out of here."

The paint horse of her dreams tried to eat the feed, but most of it dropped and dribbled out of his mouth, falling on the ground. She extended her hand to him to sniff. "I wish I had brought you peppermints. Do you remember me, Buddy?" The horse's eyes were blank, empty, and nearly lifeless. The sorry horse leaned a little and rested his muzzle by Selah's shoulder. "Don't worry, Buddy. I'm here for you, and I'm not leaving without you."

Selah turned and squared her shoulders. "Mr. Pott. You have too many horses to take care of, and I'll take him off your hands."

"That's a real purty paint horse. I'm not letting him go for nothing. He's worth at least eight fifty, but I'd be willing to take five hundred to have this nice horse go to a good home. Cash on the barrel."

"I don't have much money."

"You're trespassing on my land. If you can buy a horse, fine. If not, get off my property now."

The dogs slinked closer. One dog growled and menaced her.

"Get up, Selah." Caroline moved Dream between her and the dogs. Selah swung into the saddle. "I'll be back for him, Mr. Pott."

"Unless you have cash in your hand, don't bother me."

Neither girl had much to say on the ride back. They picked up a steady trot and set a straight course. When they rode into Grandpa's, Skunk barking was the only greeting they got.

"Where is he now?" Selah kicked her feet from the stirrups and jumped down. "Every time I look, he's gone again. I don't think he cares if I'm even here anymore. Bringing Buddy home is my last hope."

"Do you have any money?" Caroline tugged off her saddle. "I just bought a new bridle/halter combination and only have about thirty bucks left."

"I have forty-five, but I didn't bring it with me. Anyway, it's not near enough to buy Buddy."

"You could ask your grandpa or Katie."

"No and no way."

"What if there's no other way? Wouldn't your grandpa want to know his horse is half-dead? Wouldn't you want to know if it were Dream? We make a commitment to our horses for life. Even if we find them new homes, if life goes bad, we can't just look away."

"When you put it like that, you're right. If I can't pull this off, then Grandpa should know where Buddy is." Selah led the way to the kitchen and tossed Caroline a drink and a snack bar. The quiet house jarred when the clock in Grandpa's office donged four times. "Let's go see if I can find anything else helpful in Grandpa's office."

Caroline followed Selah and fiddled with a hand puzzle of a wooden elephant on his desk. "It's strange he doesn't have anything of horses in here."

"Miss Laura said he ripped horses out of his heart and out of his life. Letting me keep Dream was super hard for him. We figured out by then Dream was a foal from my grandma's horse, Harmony. That made it even harder to convince him to keep her."

Selah fingered through the files in a tall metal file cabinet. File after file of notes on horses he'd trained crammed the back of the bottom drawer. Her nose got stuffy from the old folders causing her to sneeze. As she smushed a silverfish between two papers, she noticed a file named "Coggins". She pulled it out, though she wasn't sure why. It didn't take much thumbing to find Buddy's lab tests. "Look at Buddy. He must have been two years old in this. Look how bright-eyed and alert he is. Makes me so sad to see him where he's at."

Caroline jabbed a finger on the picture at the horse's hip. "He's got a brand!"

"Yeah. So?"

"If Mr. Pott doesn't have a bill of sale to prove he bought the horse, it's legally your grandpa's."

"Caroline, you are a genius!"

"I know." She fluffed her stylish, new pixie-shag haircut with both hands.

The next morning, Grandpa had breakfast all laid out on the table for them. He sat with his coffee and morning newspaper. Folding the sports section, he enjoyed the girls tumbling into the room already dressed to ride. "I'll make you pancakes tomorrow, but cereal will have to do today. Katie wants to pick out wedding flowers this morning." He walked to the sink and poured out his cold coffee. "I can't believe I'm going flower shopping."

With her mouth full of banana, Selah muttered, "Me either."

"Are you two going to do anything else on your spring break, besides ride?"

The girls frowned confusion at each other. "Like what?" Caroline asked.

"Oh, nothing. See you girls later." He slipped on his cap.

"Please take Skunk with you so she doesn't track us. Caroline's horse is skittish about her bounding through the bushes."

Caroline's forehead wrinkled. "My mare..."

Selah kicked her under the table, and Caroline choked on her next word and glared at her.

"Skunk will love flower shopping." Grandpa's belly wiggled as he chuckled.

As they ran for the barn, Caroline asked, "Why did you tell your grandpa, my mare was afraid of Skunk?"

"Because I adore her, and if she followed us, those dogs of Mr. Pott's would tear her up."

All tacked up, the girls headed down the trail. "Oh wait." Selah trotted back to the barn. She fumbled around in the tack room, came out with a pouch, and clipped it onto the saddle. She dropped in a tall can of wasp spray.

"What's with that?"

"I watched a self-defense clinic at the trainer's expo. The teacher was a Mounted Patrol Officer. He suggested carrying wasp spray on your saddle."

"If bees attack us, the horses will fly. You won't have time to get spray out. You'll be holding on for your life."

"Not for bees. For Mr. Pott's dogs."

Caroline adjusted the strap on her lilac colored helmet embellished with the outline of a horse with flowing mane. "If you are on his property, I don't think you can spray his dogs without going to jail."

"I never realized what a great legal mind you are."

"I have a much safer and better idea. Got any hotdogs?"

Selah couldn't believe her ears. "You want to *feed* the dogs?"

"You bet. That's how burglars do it. It will work for us, too."

"Okay, if you say so." Selah dashed to the house and soon returned with two baggies full of hot dog pieces. "We better get going so we don't run out of day."

Finally, they reined in at Mr. Pott's gate.

"I'm so looking forward to the dog pack." Caroline undid the latch and swung the gate open.

"We gotta do it for Buddy."

As they approached the back of the barn, the dogs barked. The small horse herd raised their heads at the intrusion. Most went back to searching the dirt for a bite of grass, but Buddy limped toward them. Six mixed-breed dogs darted under the fence. They barked and surrounded Selah and Caroline. The girls flung hot dogs everywhere, and the dogs had a new mission. When Mr. Pott called his dogs away, they ignored him and re-sniffed the area in case they'd missed a piece. The girls relaxed in the saddles.

"You got cash?"

"We want to look the horse over before we agree to a price."

"The price is firm. If you didn't come with cash, you are trespassing, and I'm calling the sheriff."

Selah slipped from Dream's back, handed the reins to Caroline, and wiggled through the fence. As Buddy came to her, she held out a peppermint. He lipped it off her hand and put his muzzle near her ear as he munched. Throwing her arms around his neck, she buried her face in his mane. "You're coming home, Buddy. I promise."

Selah stepped to the horse's hind end. Her fingers searched in his still-thick winter coat for the brand. "My grandfather's brand is on this horse."

"It don't matter. He's on my place."

"If you don't have a bill of sale, then you have a lot of explaining to do."

"Whoa now, young lady." Mr. Pott raised one thin, bony hand. "I got the horse all fair and legal like."

"If Deputy Bob needs to come settle this, I'm sure he will agree with me."

"We don't need to call the law. Besides, I could press charges against you for trespassing."

Selah put her hands on her hips. Tucking her thumbs into empty belt loops, she glared at him.

He glowered back.

She relaxed her posture and sighed. "Mr. Pott, I'm sorry to have trespassed on your property. He was the horse my grandma always put me on before she was killed. Caroline told me he was here, and I had to see him. Now that I have, I can't leave him. I need him and he needs me."

Mr. Pott listened to her impassioned plea. "I remember your grandma. She was always nice to me—not like most folks. But I don't know why I should just give him to you when I've been taking care of him all this time."

Selah's face tightened and her jaw locked. Her eyes must have told him he was in for a fight he couldn't win because he finally dismissed her with his hand.

"Take him, if he's yours." He turned away and walked off giving a sharp whistle to his dogs.

"Thank you." Selah pulled a long, light rope from her saddlebag and fashioned a halter.

But the going was painfully slow.

"At this rate, we won't get back to your grandpa's till next week."

"I know. Every step he takes hurts me. I can't believe I am saying this, but I think we need to take him to Katie's place."

"I could ride ahead and call my dad from her farm."

"Yeah, I think you better. Ask her to think about where we can put him."

As the paint gelding attempted one more step, his head drooped almost to the ground trying to balance himself.

"I wish I could carry him." Caroline moaned as she turned her mare toward Katie's.

It felt to Selah as if they'd been baby stepping along for hours. She jerked on Buddy's halter as he dropped to his one good knee. "You can't lay down, Buddy. You might never get up again. You have to try."

Dream turned her head toward Buddy, nudged him, and then gently scratched his withers.

"Aww, you like him," she said to Dream rewarding her mare with a pat.

Finally, in the distance, a sorrel horse clipped along toward her. Dr. Steve sat in the saddle, and Caroline rode double behind him. "You didn't get far," Caroline observed.

"I'm so glad to see you. He's in bad shape."

Caroline's dad swung down and walked around the horse. "He sure went downhill fast since I saw him. He needs a shot of pain medication to start with. You can just look in his eyes and see he hurts."

"Dr. Steve, please don't tell Grandpa about the horse. He's a surprise for him."

"He'll be a surprise, all right. Why would you want to give him a horse in this condition?"

"This horse is special, but when Grandma died, Grandpa gave him away. I want him to be healthy again so I can give him back to Grandpa." *When Buddy comes home, Grandpa will remember how much he loved him. I just know it.*

Dr. Steve took the lead rope from her. "Is this your grandpa's old show horse?"

"This is Buddy." Selah dug into her saddlebag for his old photo and held it for Dr. Steve.

He shook his head as he massaged the injection site on Buddy's neck. "It will take thirty minutes for the shot to kick in, but he'll walk along a little easier." He handed the rope back to Selah and side-passed Caroline's mare next to a log where he climbed back into the saddle. Caroline swung up behind him.

"Dr. Steve, the horses at Mr. Pott's are all in bad shape. Can someone help them?"

"Caroline told me. I'll swing by and have a chat with Pott. It sounds like he is in as bad a shape as the horses."

Caroline leaned around her dad and assured Selah. "I'll be back to help."

Selah nodded. She was already deep in thought about arriving at Katie's. *I will grovel at Katie's feet if it means I can get her to take care of Buddy.*

Two long hours later, Selah and Caroline could see the roof of Katie's house. The farm had never looked so good.

Caroline's mare snatched a mouthful of tender grass as they drifted closer to Katie's. "You'll see. Katie is a tender heart, and she will love Buddy the minute she sees him."

A big breath puffed past Selah's lips. "At least you'll get to rest soon, Buddy."

As Katie came to meet them, the smile plummeted from her face, and an anguished sigh erupted from her throat. "I never imagined." She groaned. "When Caroline told me the horse needed love... I never imagined it could be this bad."

Caroline dismounted. "My dad's not optimistic about his chances."

Katie shook her head slowly from side to side. "I feel in my soul this is a creature who has given up on life." As liquid grief rushed to Katie's eyes, Selah studied her.

"Bring him to the barn in back." Katie sniffled.

"Wasn't this stall full of junk?" Selah asked, confused. "How did you move all of it?"

Katie flexed her muscles in her strongman pose. Then gestured to show off the stall swept clean of cobwebs and deeply banked in bedding. A neon-orange water bucket hung by the door, and the water sparkled like in a commercial.

"What's the smell?" Selah sniffed.

"I put peppermint essential oil in his water to encourage him to drink."

Why does she have to be so nice?

Buddy shuffled to the bucket and sniffed the water. His lips stirred it. When he slurped a deep gulp, Selah, Caroline, and Katie all smiled.

Selah's smile erased abruptly. *I wonder if this is going to backfire on me.*

CHAPTER TWELVE

*I*n the morning, on a mission to get to the barn, Selah and Caroline breezed past Grandpa in the kitchen. "Girls? I'm going to make you breakfast."

"No thanks, Grandpa. We're going riding." They grabbed several apples and rushed out.

Grandpa followed them outside holding the pancake flipper in the air. "No to blueberry pancakes. Are you on a mission?"

"We don't want to miss a single moment of riding time. Thanks, Grandpa."

"I'll be gone for a bit after lunch today." He called after them. "Katie and I are going into the bakery to taste test some wedding cakes. Fran says she makes what she calls a 'decadent' Italian crème."

Selah's motion slowed. "You don't like white cake."

"Katie does. Good enough for me."

As Selah tightened the girth, she remembered… Peppermint in his water?

The girls rocked to the rhythm of a steady trot as Katie's farm came into view. "When Buddy's all better, Grandpa can use him to teach me and Dream how to do a reining spin and a sliding stop. Soon, he will be enrolling me in school in Canaan."

"Get real."

"We're going to get Buddy all cleaned up, and he will look great. I'll be able to give him to Grandpa, and he will be so happy he'll forget all about Katie."

Caroline made a face. "Never gonna happen."

"You'll see."

After turning their horses out with the sheep, Selah and Caroline hurried to the back barn. Katie was already there. She dipped a piece of gauze into a cup and touched the crust of Buddy's eyes with tenderness. His eyelids drooped shut, and the horse didn't even move his head away. His breathing was so quiet it felt like he might be trying not to breathe. Katie cooed to him. "You're safe now." She put her hand on Buddy's face, closed her eyes, and her lips moved. The hush in the barn felt gloomy like a vase of wilted flowers.

Selah and Caroline edged closer. A twinge of guilt tugged at Selah over the way she'd treated Katie.

"I'm relieved you're here," Katie whispered. "I'm concerned about his will to live."

The girls crowded in beside him and rubbed his neck. Selah's heart clutched when she looked into his vacant eyes. "Come back, Buddy."

"My dad's here." Caroline ran from the barn to greet him.

Reaching for the dangling lead rope, Selah urged Buddy to step into the barn alleyway. He made no effort.

"He's okay right there." Dr. Steve set his bag down outside the stall and began to examine the neglected animal. "I stopped by Pott's last night. His crime is he's old and can barely take care of himself. His daughter lives in New York. I was pretty sure she had no idea what shape he's in. She's going to come check on him, and he's agreed to allow the rescue group to pick up the rest of the horses today."

Buddy's head hung to his knees as the vet ran his hands over the horse's body and down his legs. When his sunglasses fell off his head, he caught them in midair and slipped them into his vest. "My little league catcher days are finally paying off."

After a few minutes, he straightened and turned to the girls. "Here's what we've got. This guy's in rough shape. His body condition is poor. He needs IV fluids and antibiotics. His eyes and body sores need cleaning, antibiotic ointment, and daily care." He gestured toward the horse. "This swollen knee needs an injection and a liniment wrap. The front hoof problem could be a bruise, but is likely an abscess." He ran his hand over the horse's abdomen. "With this potbelly, he has an overload of parasites as well. He can barely chew. A couple of the sores in his mouth look infected. He has a cracked tooth that needs an extraction. I'd have to sedate him heavily to do the extraction surgery, and I'm concerned he may not be strong enough to bounce back."

"But he'll be all right, won't he?"

Dr. Steve stared expressionless at her for a long while before he said, "I don't think you're hearing me. A horse this malnourished has major health hurdles to overcome, and it's doubtful he can. Because of the amount of care he'd require, he would need to be moved to my clinic. That's a major expense. I know you don't want to hear this, but I wouldn't be doing my job if I didn't tell you his prognosis is poor."

"No!" Selah and Caroline gasped.

Selah frowned. "Are you saying you think we should put him down? Because that's the way it sounds...." Her voice trailed off.

Katie stepped from the shadows. "Under no circumstances will we give up on this horse even if he's given up on himself. We will fight for him until he can fight with us."

The girls gawked at Katie, stunned to silence by the power in her voice.

Dr. Steve took a step backward. "Yes, ma'am. Let's get busy then, shall we?"

Long after Buddy woke from sedation for his dental work, he lay stretched out in his stall. Selah sat in the stall bedding, cradling his head. Caroline finger massaged him. The two friends talked to and encouraged the horse.

"My dad did everything he could, but Buddy doesn't seem to want to try." Caroline moved her hands over the horse. "I hope rubbing will help him understand we love him."

"How am I ever going to be able to pay for everything your dad's doing?"

"Well, you get the 'my best friend' discount. And my dad said we could help with the 4H group coming to the clinic next weekend. Plus, I heard Katie tell Dad she would help with expenses." Caroline extended a stalk of tender grass hay toward Buddy. "You're so lucky Katie's going to be your new grandma."

Selah ran her fingers through Buddy's forelock. "Could you believe how she stood up for Buddy?"

"I know. I wish she was going to be my grandma."

"Some lunch, anyone?" Katie carried a covered plate of sandwiches into the barn and set them on a hay bale. "I've got to go for a bit. Caroline, if you'll come with me, I'll show you where my special formula bran mash is that I made for Buddy."

Trotting along behind Katie, Caroline asked, "What's bran mash?"

"Bran that's been soaked in boiling water. But mine has probiotics for his gut and molasses for sweetness. He should gobble it right up."

With one finger, Selah traced the bony structure of Buddy's face and stroked his rough hair. "Do you remember when you would follow me around like you were my puppy? You were my first love, and I'll love you forever." She hugged his face. "I look at the picture of you and me together and dream of riding you again. Look at you now. This is so not fair. Now that I've found you, I'm going to do everything I can, but you have to help." Selah's tears darkened Buddy's coat, but the horse still made no effort to rise.

"It's been a long time," Selah questioned Caroline. "Do you think Buddy should be getting up by now?"

Caroline stood and rolled the tightness out of her shoulders. "I do. He'd recovered from the sedation before my dad left. Let's ask him to get up." Caroline clucked encouragement.

Selah tugged on the halter. "I'm afraid he's given up. We've got to get him on his feet."

The horse opened his eyes but acted like he couldn't care less. Selah pulled harder. Caroline clucked louder. She grabbed an old walking stick out of a bucket in the corner and tapped his hip.

Buddy startled at the tap of the stick, lifted his head, and sat awkwardly up.

"Keep tapping. It's getting him to think about moving," Selah ordered, keeping steady pressure on his lead rope.

Buddy heaved himself to his feet.

Selah breathed a sigh of great relief. "Good for you, sweet boy."

"Dad said we should feed him the bran mash Katie made as soon as he is awake enough." Caroline sprinted to the feed room and got a cup of the mash.

"That's all?"

"Katie said he can only handle a little at a time."

Selah's voice raised an octave, "Katie raises sheep. What does she know about horses?"

"More than you think. Do you know how to make mash?"

Selah turned away and brushed Buddy. Caroline took up her position, brushing on the other side of the horse, who ignored his feed bucket.

"He's not interested." Caroline squeezed her eyes shut. "What horse doesn't eat mash?"

"He's got to eat or he's going to die." Selah opened his mouth and wiped some mash on the inside of his cheek with her fingers. The paint horse didn't respond to her efforts.

"I hope Katie comes back soon. She'll have an idea."

Selah chucked the brush into a nearby bucket. "This isn't going the way I planned."

Selah and Caroline spent day after day of their spring break in Katie's barn.

"He's still so lifeless. He doesn't even move around. Flies land on him, and he doesn't bother to swish his tail," Selah moaned. "I can't convince him to eat anything."

"We've been stroking and talking to him for days, and he still acts like he's here by himself." Caroline frowned. "What's going to happen when we go back to school tomorrow?"

The following Tuesday afternoon, Selah barely walked in the door after school when the phone rang. Katie blurted, "There's no change in Buddy. If anything, he's worse. He stands with his eyes drooped closed. He won't eat mash or beet pulp. I've offered him carrots and apples, but he leaves them in the bucket. I tried giving him one of my older ewes as a companion, but I think he depressed her. She stands next to him with the same look of utter despair."

"Maybe let him out to eat grass?"

"He'll look out at the grass, but he stands in the open stall door and doesn't move for hours. I think he needs a job. Needs a reason to be important. I was thinking about riding him."

"You? Have you ever ridden a horse?"

"Yes, me. I'm the only one here. No, I've never been on a horse."

"Well, it's too late to start now." Selah huffed. "He's too weak anyway. His muscles aren't strong enough. He might fall and crush you."

"He's not going to crush me. I was hoping you could tell me what to do."

"Over the phone?" she squeaked her disbelief.

"What could be easier than turning over a bucket and using it to get on him?"

"Falling off! Falling off would be easier."

"Maybe, you're right. Maybe, we should tell your grandpa. He might know what to do to help Buddy."

"No, no, no. You cannot tell Grandpa. If Buddy dies, it will be better if Grandpa never knew about him."

"I don't agree.... I have an idea. I gotta run. Bye."

"Wait. What idea? Miss Katie? Katie!"

Selah called back to Katie's farm every day after school, but Katie never answered. "What century does she live in that there is no way to leave her a message? I guess, if she rode Buddy and fell off, Grandpa would have found them by now. I told her not to."

On Friday, Grandpa arrived to chauffeur her to the farm. Selah watched him for any hint he'd discovered her secret.

"Did you have a good week?" he asked.

"It was okay."

"What time do you have to be at the vet clinic tomorrow?"

"Before nine a.m."

"It was nice of you to volunteer to help with the 4H group."

"It was the least I could do."

"What do you mean?"

"Oh, nothing. Caroline's a great friend, and I'm happy to help her. Are you hanging out with Katie tomorrow?"

"I don't know." His forehead wrinkled. "She's been busy and not telling me what she's up to. I think she's working on wedding plans."

"A few weeks is not very long. Maybe you should postpone it. You know—to give her more time to plan."

"Not a chance!" Grandpa turned into the farm driveway.

Selah's group of third-grade, 4H kids huddled around, plying her with questions about horses. She taught them everything she knew about grooming a horse, including sharing her technique for adding pink highlights to their mane and tail.

Too soon, Selah and Caroline waved goodbye to the vanload of kids. Before the dust settled, Selah asked, "Dr. Steve, on the way home could we drop by Miss Katie's to see how Buddy's doing? I haven't talked to her since Tuesday, and Katie was super worried about him."

"I was out there Tuesday, and he was pretty much the same. But it's on the way."

"Thank you, Dr. Steve."

"Thank you, Miss Selah, for coming out today to help. You were great with the kids. I heard them getting loud and then realized you had them laughing."

"I had fun with them. They love horses and I love horses."

Dr. Steve slowed as a young buck popped out of the bushes by the side of the road. "The best was the stick horse show classes you did with them. You need to plan on helping me next year because they'd be disappointed otherwise."

Caroline said, "You're a good sport, Dad. I got video of you cantering a stick horse."

"Oh no." He groaned.

As they drove to Katie's barn, all heads turned with eyes wide open. "*What* is she doing?" Selah gulped.

Dr. Steve chuckled. "Looks like she put him to work. I didn't know he was broke to a cart."

"He's not! She can't be serious."

As Selah rushed to Buddy, a smile bubbled up from her toes. "His lights are on!"

Katie walked beside the cart and flicked the reins to drive Buddy forward.

"Where did you get a cart?" Selah's eyes bulged.

"The cart and an old harness were in a tool shed. My late-husband used to have a horse he drove many years ago."

"How did you get Buddy trained to pull it? I've only been gone six days."

"You have to train them to pull a cart? I thought he just knew what to do." She shrugged. "I put the harness on and backed him to the cart. It took me forever to figure out how all the straps hooked together. I borrowed a trick of your grandpa's and duct taped the poles into the loops on the side. Buddy waited patiently and slept on his feet most of the time. At first, he didn't like the cart chasing him, but he's all good with it now."

"Do you have any idea how dangerous it is to hook an untrained horse to a cart? It's a wonder he didn't panic and kill you both." Selah shook her head. "Duct tape."

Dr. Steve put his hand on Selah's shoulder and changed the subject. "So, how did you get him to start eating?"

"I made him applesauce with brown sugar and put it in a syringe. I squirted a tiny bit into his mouth every hour and gave him a good rubdown. Before you know it, he was nickering for more." Katie giggled like a schoolgirl. "Then I mixed the applesauce in small amounts of his bran mash. Once he started eating, he perked up some but still seemed so depressed. So I gave him a job to do. His muscles are very weak, but I thought he could pull a light cart. I can move it easily. I decided to lead rather than to drive him so he wouldn't be pulling my weight. He seemed to enjoy our adventure. We ambled around the lamb's pasture, and I loaded the sticks and limbs blown down in the last storm."

Selah angled away from Katie and talked into Caroline's ear. "Could this turn out bad for me? You know how dangerous it is to hook a thousand-pound panic-ohalic to a cart, but Katie didn't. When Grandpa hears what she did, he will be furious at me for putting Katie in danger and then love her more for saving Buddy."

Caroline raised her eyebrows and nodded. "You're going to have to make sure he doesn't know anything about this for a long time."

CHAPTER THIRTEEN

When Grandpa's phone rang, Selah lifted *The Black Stallion* book she'd fallen asleep reading from her chest and fumbled to answer it. "Hello?"

The voice on the other end of the phone cried, "Selah, is your grandpa home?"

She rubbed her eyes. "No, ma'am. He went to town."

"Oh dear, oh dear. What to do?"

"What's wrong, Miss Katie?" Her book slipped from her hand and lost her place. "Is Buddy worse?"

"It's not Buddy. I found the gate open. I must have forgotten to close it after Buddy and I got the sticks out of the pasture this afternoon. My ewes with lambs got out and have wandered off."

Selah's fingers pinched one cheek, and her eyes widened. "Oh no. The babies."

"I'm so worried. I'm sure they got out into The Grasslands. I've called for them and hunted everywhere. It's already too dark to search."

"He should be home soon. He'll call you back," she promised and hung up. She rested her forehead on the window glass and watched the long, dark driveway.

Finally, a dim light. Selah rushed out the door onto the porch. It seemed to her, Grandpa was driving slower than a horse could walk backward.

The minute he parked, Selah hurried to him. "Grandpa, you need to call Miss Katie right away."

"Is she all right?" His face reflected his concern.

"She's very upset about her lambs."

"Grab the groceries, would you?" He went directly to the phone.

She got all the groceries put away before he hung up. He stood staring out the window with his back to her.

"So, have the ewes come home?"

"No. Katie is beside herself with worry. I told her I'd come at first light and help her look."

"Should we go over there and be with her?"

"I asked her that, and she said 'no, in the morning would be fine'." He tilted his head and searched Selah's face. "I'm happy to see the old Selah in your response to Katie's problem."

Selah lowered her eyes and concentrated on her hands. "I'm having a little trouble learning how to be a teenager." She smoothed and re-smoothed the plastic grocery bags. "There are two of me arguing in my head. It's noisy and crowded. One of them is always upset and nagging at me."

"Ah. Sounds like the age-old battle between putting yourself first or not."

Selah sighed deeply. "I want the good in me to win."

"Then you'll need to fight that battle in prayer."

She whipped around to peer out the window into the darkness when a coyote yipped nearby. "I hope the coyote pack is busy far from Katie's tonight."

"Boy, so do I. They would wipe out every one of her new lambs. She can't believe she forgot to close the gate. Her mind must be somewhere else. It's just not like her." He shook his head, and his face wrinkled in a puzzled way, crinkling his forehead.

Yeah, her mind is on Buddy. This's my fault. "Dream and I can help."

He started to shake his head no but stopped and considered her. "Guess it wouldn't do me any good to tell you to stay home. You'd be out there lookin' anyway." He hugged her. "Guess I love that about you. If someone needs help, you're in line."

"If anybody can find the sheep, Dream and I can."

"You might be right."

Selah clutched the smoothed bags and peered out the window into the darkness. "How long can the new mammas go without water?"

"I don't know much about sheep. It would depend on what they're eating, and fresh grass has a high water content."

"I think we need to find them fast because the mamas would need water to make milk for the babies." Selah creased and folded shopping bags into little triangles.

"Good point. Got to be water out there. Dream made it two years, and she didn't do it by inhaling water vapor."

"But it's her secret," Selah reminded him.

"Why do you do that?" Grandpa took the neatly folded shopping bags from her. "Too much neatness for me."

She shrugged.

"Is your saddle pack ready?"

"Always."

"Good, I need to double check mine. I've been lazy about restocking it after the search for Ellie." He hauled his backpack out of the closet and plopped it on the table.

"I have an idea, Grandpa. What if Dream gets thirsty overnight? Then I could ride into The Grasslands and let Dream have her head. She might take me to the water."

"Well, what if she did? We don't know anything about where the sheep went."

"Shouldn't they go back to Katie's when they get thirsty?"

"Any other animal would, but sheep are a mite stupid. But if you remove her water, you need to remove her hay, too, so she doesn't colic. She's got some grass in her paddock to keep her busy for the night."

"I'll go right now and take her water bucket out of her stall." The back door shut before the whole sentence made it out of her mouth. A nicker drifted from the dark paddock. "This is going to look crazy to you. Just trust me, okay? It's important you take me to your water hole tomorrow." Selah pulled the bucket off the hook and dumped most of the water. The horse dipped her nose into her almost-dry bucket. "Sorry, girl. I have to. I left you a little. After what Katie's done for Buddy, we have to help her. If we don't find those lambs, the coyotes will."

Selah dropped off to sleep already dressed to ride.

It was still dark when Grandpa rattled her door. "I'm up," she called as her feet hit the floor. When she got outside, Grandpa already had Sweet Dream tacked up. He tucked snack bars into her saddlebag and hung water on both sides of the saddle. A coiled rope was tied to the saddle D ring.

"I've decided to take Skunk with me. You have a knife in your vest?" he asked.

"Yes."

"And your GPS?"

"Like I don't know my way around?"

Grandpa looked at her over a nonexistent pair of reading glasses and frowned. "Get going then. Be careful out there. Don't take any chances. I want you back at the farm no later than four o'clock—no matter what." He handed her a radio. "I put fresh batteries in your walkie-talkie. Check in with me."

"Got it."

Selah shaded her eyes from the sun directly overhead and scanned the field. "I'd like to see sheep about now."

She held the button down on the walkie-talkie. "Grandpa, can you hear me?"

"You must have read my mind. Katie and I were just wondering if you were having better luck than we are."

"No, I haven't seen any sign of the sheep."

"We followed their tracks for a good mile, but we lost their trail."

"Dream must be a camel and not need water."

"Be patient and keep looking. We're going to keep moving west."

Selah clicked the radio off and sat as still as possible in the saddle. Not touching the reins, she kept the horse moving but allowed the mare to make the decisions about which way to go. "Come on, Dream. You've got to be thirsty."

Just as Selah was about to give up, Dream smacked her lips. The mare swerved into heavy brush. Branches slapped Selah's face, and she couldn't see the trail. Masses of sticky cobwebs plastered her forehead, cheeks, and shoulders, and she flailed her arms. "Ick! Double ick!" Right in front of her hung a tree branch about six inches in diameter. "Oops, I'm in trouble. Whoa, whoa, *whoa!*"

Dream wasn't interested in whoa.

As the branch swept Selah from the saddle, she clung to it.

The horse walked away with an empty saddle. When Selah dropped to the ground absorbing the concussion in her knees, Dream stopped and turned her head to look back at Selah.

"Are you laughing at me?" Holding tight to Dream's tail, Selah shuffled her feet trying to keep up. They traipsed through thick brush for another thirty feet before the path widened to a clearing. Filtered sunlight sparkled across Dream's hidden pond. Tiny duckweed leaves floated on the murky water like a thick green carpet.

Dream alerted in an instant to the strange creatures at her watering hole. The ewes bleated to them. "Wonder how many should be here?" A quick headcount came up with seven ewes, but only four lambs. One mama and baby stood in the water.

"Grandpa, can you hear me?" Selah let the button up on the radio and waited. "Selah to Grandpa! Oh great, now what?"

At first, she thought the two sheep in the middle of the pond were drinking. As time passed, and they didn't move, she began to wonder. "I can tell you for sure sloshing out there is not an option. I'm not ruining my boots to save your fleeces."

She climbed into the saddle and walked the mare a few steps into the water. The ewe struggled to get away, but she was stuck fast in the mud. "Oh no, you guys aren't going anywhere, are you?"

Selah gulped. A black snake coiled at the edge of the water watched her. It stretched upward with a hiss. When its mouth gaped open, fangs highlighted by its white throat flashed a threat.

With her heart pounding in her chest, she wiped sweaty hands on her jeans. "Go away."

Best not to aggravate a cottonmouth. "I'm keeping my eyes on you. Nasty thing."

She pressed the button and tried again to reach Grandpa. "There's a nasty snake here. Grandpa? This radio is worthless. Grandpa? A phone might work better. Grandpa? Never mind."

She chucked it into the saddlebag.

Focusing on the immediate problem, she pondered what to do. "This rope is way limp. How am I to show off my cowgirl rope-throwing skills with a lame rope?" Selah twirled the saggy rope. "It's up to you, Dream." She nudged Dream to take one step and then another until she felt them sink into the mud. "Far enough." She stretched forward in the saddle and pitched a loop toward the ewe. It fell short. On her second try, the rope settled over her head. The mama bleated and struggled against the rope. Thrashing its body side to side broke the suction. Dream's feet sucked out of the heavy mud as she backed out of the water pulling the mama sheep.

"Your turn next," Selah warned the trapped lamb. She remounted Dream, and they eased into the water. She tossed the loop and missed a couple times. When she cued Dream to take one more step, the mare flipped her nose and refused. Selah drew her knees up underneath herself in the saddle and stretched over the horse's neck. Her throw found its mark, but she lost her balance. She grabbed for the saddle horn as she flipped. She tumbled and splashed into the dark, slimy water. Dream sucked away from the commotion. Selah landed on her jeans pockets facing the horse.

She wallowed in the mud with her armpits at the water line and glanced at the lamb next to her. "See what you did? This is the kind of trouble Grandpa told me to stay out of."

Selah pushed against the gooey pond bottom and struggled to stand. The bog was so thick; it wouldn't let her go. She searched the bank for the coiled snake. *What's that ripple under the water?* "Get away from me, snake."

Trying not to panic, she shifted and strained to get her feet underneath her. "This isn't working!"

Dream waited at the edge of the water and tilted her head watching Selah.

"I know what you're thinking. Don't you dare leave me, Dream." Selah made kissing sounds to Sweet Dream—her cue to come forward.

The horse responded with a small step.

"I need you, Dream. You've got to come to me. If you leave me here, no one will ever find me." Selah kept kissing, and Dream took tiny, obedient, but reluctant steps into the bog. The mud glopped thick around her hooves. "You can't come any farther, can you? Or we'll both be mired here." Selah reached toward the dangling stirrup, but it hung miles out of reach. She closed her eyes and sighed. "I need a little help here."

The mare's nose brushed her cheek. She clutched mane with her free hand and held on. The horse flung her head high and heaved a step back, wrenching Selah from the bog. When her other hand freed, she threw her arm around Dream's neck. Dream backed out of the mire with a muddy, dripping Selah dangling around her neck. As she set her feet on solid ground, she patted the mare. "You're the best, Dream."

The rope around the lamb's neck floated out of reach. "I'm not going in after you. I'm not leaving you to die either." Selah scoured the nearby woods to find a long branch. Slapping the water with the stick, she finally hooked the rope and worked the end toward shore. Looping the rope around the saddle horn, they stepped backward and tugged. "This lamb is too weak to help." The lamb didn't thrash, and the suction held it tight. "Hum… Break your neck or let you die in the mud? We have to take the chance!" She cued the horse to step back, hauling on the rope and gradually increasing the tension. Then the lamb popped from the quagmire's grip. It flopped on its side and slipped under the water surface. Selah and Dream hurried, dragging the lamb through the water like a wooly fish caught in a net. When they hauled it free of the water, Selah sprung to its side. One of its legs looked mangled, and the lamb wasn't breathing. She pushed energetically on the lamb's rib cage. Nothing happened. "I risked my neck for you. Breathe!"

Throwing all her weight behind one huge effort, Selah thumped on the lamb's rib cage. The little lamb coughed up water and filled its lungs with air. "This is for you, Katie." She pointed her finger to the sky.

Its mama came to its side and bleated. Pond ooze drained from its lungs and smeared on Selah. "Puke!"

The ewe butted the weak lamb with her nose. Selah bent over the baby and looped her arms around it to hold up its head. "You're even too weak to suckle. We have to get you to Miss Katie quick."

She heaved the fragile lamb up behind the saddle. Dream turned to look at her odd, sludge-covered passenger. As the mud dripped down her flanks, the mare flipped her head but stood still. Selah worked to tie the lamb onto the saddle. Not sure her knots would hold, she dug into her saddlebag. "Grandpa, I love you." She lifted out a roll of pink duct tape. Ripping off some long pieces, she wrapped the baby's feet securely and bound them to the saddle.

They backtracked down the overgrown path to the meadow where Selah mounted and headed Dream to Miss Katie's farm. The muck in her pants oozed down her legs. Water sloshed in her boots, and silt squished between her toes. "My boots are so ruined. You're a lot of trouble, baby." Once clear of the trees, Selah took a deep breath and tried the radio. "Oh. Ugh. I had the mute button on. No wonder it wouldn't work." She wiped grime off the radio onto the saddle blanket. "Selah to Grandpa. Do you hear me?"

"We hear you, Selah. What's wrong with your radio? We could hear rustling, but you were not responding to our questions. What's your status?"

"I had a technical problem—I need a phone." She paused to let it sink in. "I found seven ewes and four lambs. I'm leading them to Katie's now."

"We'll head home to meet you."

"Okay." *Home? He calls Katie's place home?*

The lamb's mama ran closely behind Dream, and the rest of the herd followed along, too.

Selah's hand rested on the soggy, wooly bundle behind her saddle. The lamb's head drooped, and she only heard it sputter an occasional cough.

Katie, in her bright-yellow flowered shirt, stood with Grandpa near the barn. Her tears flooded her eyes and poured down her cheeks. She covered her face with her hands. Grandpa put his arm around her and hugged her to his chest. When she leaned onto him, her smile outshone her tears, but it didn't stop them.

Maybe I've been too hard on her. She loves sheep like I love horses.
Selah's eyes filled with tears. She slid from Sweet Dream's back, and Katie pulled her into a crushing hug, filth and all.

When Selah remembered her helpless cargo behind the saddle, Grandpa was already cutting the weak little passenger free. She flipped open her knife and helped him cut away the duct tape and rope. He lifted the limp lamb and carried it to the sheep barn. The bleating mama followed her baby. Katie hustled to the house for dry towels and clean bottles. For a long while, she didn't say anything except sweet nothings to her lamb. She dried the lamb's coat, set up a heat lamp, and coaxed milk down its throat. He ushered the rest of her flock into their pasture and secured the gate. *Grandpa does seem to be at home here.*

"Grandpa hasn't seen Buddy, has he?" Selah whispered to Katie.

"No, I locked him into the barn today." Katie put her hand on Selah's arm. "Thank you for going to look for my lambs. I love these little guys, and it breaks my heart to lose even one. Because of you, I got most of them back." Her voice dropped to a hush. "I'm very grateful."

"This is all my fault. I'm so sorry."

"Your fault? I left the gate open."

Selah peered furtively around for Grandpa. "Only because you're so busy with you-know-what. Anyway, I'm sorry."

Katie stopped. Her eyes were soft and kind as she listened to Selah.

"It's been hard for me because I thought, if it weren't for you, I could move to the farm when my family moves to Austin. But... watching you with Buddy... I realize I might be wrong about some things. Maybe a lot of things."

Grandpa walked toward them.

"I know you have to go," Katie said. "We can talk more next weekend. Time always makes things clear."

CHAPTER FOURTEEN

*D*ad's keys lay spread on the kitchen counter.

"Dad's home first, again?" Selah plopped her backpack on the floor and grabbed a snack bar. With a mouth full of chocolate chips, oatmeal, and peanut butter, she picked her way through the maze of packing boxes.

If Dad heard her come into the room, he didn't look up from the computer screen. Selah eased up behind him and set her chin on his shoulder.

"It's a professional network where I've posted my resume and job experience."

"I thought your job in Austin was a lock?"

"So did I. The financing fell through. There is no buyout."

"No Austin? Do you get to keep working at your old company until someone else buys it?" She couldn't keep the delight from her voice.

He shook his head and sighed. "No, I'm closing down my last project, and the company shuts down next week. On the bright side, you don't have to worry about moving to Austin anymore." He shut the laptop and walked through the alley of book cartons toward the door. He paused in the doorway. "How would you like to go to the biggest amusement park on the West Coast?"

"You bet."

"Glad we finally found an idea you like. A company based in San Diego expressed interest in hiring me a couple weeks ago, but the buyout was still viable then. I did a real-time interview, and they're overnighting an airline ticket for my final interview."

Selah couldn't breathe. "In California? I'll never see Dream again for the rest of my life!"

"The logistics do present a problem. I won't lie. We're going to have to make the best of it." He tried to smile. "Your grandpa is on his way to get you for a lesson with Jordan—better get ready."

In a trance-like state, she trudged up the stairs to get her things. As she started to zip her backpack, she noticed her devotional notebook tucked in with her schoolbooks. She opened it to the last entry from about a year ago. Clicking her pink pen, she wrote: Dear God. I can't do this anymore. Please help me.

Selah waited on the sidewalk by the curb for Grandpa, her brain numb from trying to figure out what to do. If Dad got the job in California, she would lose everything. Starting with every friend she'd ever had. Vanessa had dumped her once—she wouldn't even notice if Selah wasn't there one day. Amanda already had tons of friends—she wouldn't miss Selah, either. Caroline was so nice— she would find a friend to replace her in a flash. *I will only have*

friends on Facelook. They will post all their happy horse pictures, and I will heart them and feel lousy.

Austin is three hours from the farm, but California is three *days*. A thunderstorm rumbled nearby. Selah chilled as the wind picked up and the temperature dipped into the 60s.

Dream would forget everything we'd ever taught her. I would only see her once a year at Christmas.

"Grandpa will have Katie, and he won't even miss me." She looked around to see if anyone was watching her talk to herself, but the street was quiet.

A light rush of raindrops splattered around her. Dark clouds crowded overhead. Before she could decide to race for the house, Grandpa's blue truck turned the corner. "Hurry, Grandpa. I'm about to drown here."

Pulling the truck door open, she leaped in with her stuff. "One more minute and..."

A deluge of rain drowned out her voice, and she gave up. The rain pounded the truck and then slacked off as quickly as it started.

"Perfect timing." Grandpa patted her knee. "Nice to see you."

"There is no perfect anything."

"Or maybe not. You sound like your dad told you the Austin job fell through."

Selah nodded and stared at the rounded toes of her boots.

"I can't put a good spin on it. I'm glad he's got a job possibility because times are tough in the job market right now, but California changes everything."

"I'll never get to see you."

"It's gonna be tough on everyone. But your dad's got to have a job."

She hung her head. "If I lived at the farm, at least I'd still have you and Dream. I could help more with chores. But I would never see my family. I'm kidding myself to think I can leave them. I love my family, and it would hurt my little brothers so much. I'm not even looking for a good answer anymore—there just isn't one."

Grandpa glanced over at her and then back at the road. He pulled off into the Bo's Steak And Ribs parking lot and turned off the motor.

"Why are we stopping? We never eat here."

"I have something I have to tell you before we get to the farm."

She widened her eyes, sensing more bad news.

"The farm chores are getting to be a bit much for me, especially since I've been helping Katie with her farm." He looked straight ahead.

Selah's mouth slipped into high gear. "Yeah. I could be a big help. I'm old enough to learn to drive the mower. I wouldn't mind at all. And I could take over all the chores for Skunk, Pearl, and Dream. I could help with your computer and smartphone stuff. We could get me a smartphone, and I could talk to my family every day. There is this awesome cool app where you can, like, video text."

He scratched the top of his forehead and ran his hand down over his face. "I appreciate your willingness. There's no good time to tell you, so I'm just going to lay it out." He placed his hand on top of hers. "Truthfully, I'm thinking it might be time to sell the farm. I'm rattling around in my big old house. The repairs are getting the best of me, and the taxes are only going up."

Her mouth dropped open, and she jerked her hand away.

"Sell the farm?" Selah's face contorted. Her forehead scrunched in a major frown.

Her lips began to tremble. Her tongue all but hung from her mouth while it drooped open, and she turned in slow motion as the worst news of all dawned on her. "Dream! Where would

Dream stay? Dad said we can't afford board for a horse. Could Dream stay at Katie's?"

"You don't understand. We're going to sell both farms. Katie and I want to travel."

Shock tightened Selah's throat. She took small, quick breaths, and the weight of a boulder pressed on her chest.

"Maybe you should sell Dream."

She gasped for breath. "Sell my heart!" Her voice cracked, and her head wobbled no. "Can you imagine the moment when I have to hand her lead rope to some other girl?" Both hands in the air, she clenched her fists. "She would lead my horse to her trailer, shut the door, and drive away." She beat her fists on an air drum. "What would Dream think? That I'd betrayed her." Selah pressed her palms into her eye sockets and shook her head violently.

"Once you're settled in California, you could get a new horse. Maybe find one without any loose screws."

Selah couldn't believe her ears. How could Grandpa sell the farm? How could he think, for even a moment, that she could ever part with Dream? "My parents said we couldn't afford board when we were talking about living in Austin. California would be a hundred times more." Selah rode the rest of the trip to the farm in shocked silence.

The next morning, Selah struggled to focus on her lesson with Jordan. As Sweet Dream walked away from Selah, she threw her hands up. "I can't do this. I can't do anything."

"When you take off the halter, all you have between you is the truth about your relationship." Jordan pulled the halter and lead rope from the fence of Grandpa's arena and handed them to Selah. "Your heart isn't in this today. For you to learn how to handle Dream at liberty not only do I need your focused attention, but Dream needs you to be all in the game."

"Sorry, Jordan, you're right." Selah dug her toe in the dirt and wiggled it around. "It doesn't seem to matter anymore. My dad got a job."

"Austin is not so bad. We can make it work."

"His new job is in California!"

"Oh, that's rough."

"On top of that, suddenly I find out Grandpa's selling the farm. Can you even believe it? What a nightmare! Where would he live, I'd like to know?"

"It's his farm and his life."

"Selling it ruins everything." She closed her eyes and tilted her head back. "How would I pay to board her? She can't live in Katie's overloaded sheep pasture because they are selling Katie's farm, too." Selah stomped her foot. "Grandpa suggested I sell her. If I have to ride her all the way to California—I will."

"Sell her? We'll think of something." Jordan rested a hand on Selah's shoulder.

"Right. Did you see the real estate sign in front of the farm?"

"Hard to miss a red-and-white sign that big. Sorry. I know it hurts."

"The farm always felt like it was mine, too." Selah stared at Grandpa off in the distance on his four-wheeler. "What I want doesn't matter to anybody. What does selling the farm say about the time I've spent here with him? This part of my life is over— just like that? Gone like it never mattered."

"I imagine he'd like to do other things besides farm chores. Did you know he always wanted to go to Israel?"

Selah shook her head. "Not until yesterday."

"We were talking about the amazing sunrise and the glory of Creation this morning before you came out. He told me he dreamed of going to Israel because he wanted to walk on holy ground."

"The Grasslands is holy ground." Tears ran down Selah's cheeks. "I was getting used to the idea of Grandpa getting married soon, but I never dreamed he'd sell our farm and leave. I wish I could see into the future to see how my life will work out. It's all I can think about. It all looks hopeless, and it keeps getting worse."

Jordan pulled her into a hug.

Selah's voice choked. "I found Grandpa's paint horse." She wiped her tears on the hem of her T-shirt as Dream stuck her head between them. Selah rubbed little circles on Dream's shoulder.

"You did? That's wonderful. You've wanted to find him so bad."

"It's too late, and it's not working out like I'd hoped. He's been neglected and in really bad shape. I could only get him as far as Katie's farm. She's taking care of him. Guess who will look like an angel to Grandpa? Hint. It won't be me."

"Was finding the paint horse really for your grandpa?"

"I thought finding him could change everything for both of us. But where is Grandpa going to keep Buddy if he sells the farm?"

Jordan bent to look her in the eyes. "It will all work out somehow. You'll see. I've been through tough stuff like this, remember? Focus on the step you have to take right in front of you." Jordan walked her to the arena gate. "For this moment, you have a commitment to do The Classan Ranch Benefit in five weeks. You both have the talent, but you don't have much time to get this together. Work with her and concentrate on the exercises, and it will keep your mind off things you can't control anyway."

"Yes, Mother."

"Since I know your mother, I'm going to take that as a compliment." Jordan hugged Selah again. "I gotta hit the road. Go ride the trails. That always makes you feel better."

"If I ever get the paint horse home, you could ride with me. But by then, it doesn't look like this will be home." Selah waved with half a heart to Jordan.

While she rode Dream on the trail through The Grasslands, Selah's mind whirled. "What're we going to do, Dream? What is going to happen to us? I've got nothing left to try. I'm still moving. Just now, it's to another country. California doesn't even touch Texas. And Grandpa's going to marry Katie and sell our farm. Every time I think it can't get worse, it does." A flash of light and a crack of thunder jolted the calm air.

Selah's eyes fluttered open for a moment. "Why am I lying in the dirt?" she muttered weakly. "Why am I all wet?"

A beetle crawled past her nose.

"Skunk, you need to brush your teeth." She tried to push the dog's cold nose out of her face. "You have doggy breath."

Not wanting to move, Selah closed her eyes again, craving sleep, except Skunk nudged and licked her face to the point of being a major nuisance. Selah shifted around a little, still face down. She moved her arms an inch and then her legs. "Everything seems to work." She struggled to sit up. "Except my head." She scooted in slow motion to a tree and leaned her back against it. Unbuckling her helmet, she let the strap hang. "Dream? Where are you? You traitor!

The going gets rough, and you leave me out here!" Selah tried to wipe the mud off her face and arms, but the grime just smeared. Her bright-pink T-shirt was now a dirty-rose color.

"It rained? Wasn't the sun out? What in the world happened, Skunk?"

Starting to feel stronger, Selah eased herself to her knees, leaning against the tree. The dizziness seemed to pass, until it hadn't, and she slid back to the ground. "Grandpa must be getting worried. If Dream went home, he's probably called out the National Guard."

Skunk continued to check, lick, and poke on Selah. "You've been living with Grandpa too long. You're a worrywart just like him."

In the distance, a blue mirage floated toward her. As she struggled to think, it dawned on Selah—it was Grandpa on his four-wheeler. Grateful and tired, she raised her arm and tried to wave.

"Selah?"

"I don't know, Grandpa." Propping herself on the tree, she stood. When she swayed, he jumped off and gripped her elbow.

"It's a two-hundred-dollar fine to have a motorized vehicle out here."

"Fine or no fine. I had to find you. Dream must have galloped the whole way home. She was all lathered up. What happened?"

"We were walking along the trail, and then I don't remember." She pulled her helmet off and tucked it under her arm.

"Do you think you can ride?" He took the helmet from her and scrutinized the jagged crack exposing its foam core.

"I think." She leaned on him as she lifted her foot over the seat. When he slipped into the driver's seat, she wrapped her arms around him and rested her head on his back. "I'm so sleepy, but if I close my eyes, my head starts to spin."

Skunk jumped into her traveling position behind Selah and stuck her nose on Selah's shoulder.

Grandpa held tightly to her hands clasped over his belly so she didn't slip from him. "Keep your eyes open and tell me if you think you can't," he instructed as he started the engine and drove smoothly off. "Talk about anything, sunshine. Tell me how you're coming with the liberty work. Tell me about your blog."

As they neared the house, Selah nodded off, and Skunk licked her ear.

Grandpa stopped and killed the motor. He glanced at Dream, still tacked up, standing in her paddock. He scooped Selah up and carried her to the truck.

"I can walk, Grandpa!" she objected, but her head sagged onto his shoulder.

"Of course, you can, sunshine." Pulling a seatbelt around her and clipping it, he smiled, but his eyes looked worried. "I'd feel better if you had some sparkle to your eyes, and I'll be grateful to get you to the hospital."

He called the vet's office. "I need to talk to Callie, right away, please." He shut the door to the truck. "Callie, there's been an accident. I'm on the way to the emergency room with Selah. Can you come out to the house right away and take care of Dream? She's overheated, needs her tack pulled, and check her right front." In quick strides, he hurried around the truck. "If you think she needs Dr. Steve to look at her, tell him what's going on."

"I'm on my way, Ed."

"Thanks." After climbing into the truck, he slammed the door. The truck wheels spun and gravel flew. As the truck surged forward, Selah glanced in the side mirror at her faithful dog, standing alert, watching them go.

Grandpa dialed and handed the phone to Selah. "Talk to your daddy, sunshine. Tell him what happened."

"Hi, Daddy."

"To what do I owe the honor of your phone call?"

"I'm sleepy, and Grandpa is making me talk to stay awake."

"What!"

"I'm okay, but I don't know what happened. There was a big flash of light. Dream leaped to the side. I can't remember anything else. Grandpa's taking me to see Dr. Amy. He wants to know if you and Mom will meet us there. Grandpa just cut somebody off when he pulled onto the highway. They are honking and waving."

Outside the emergency room door, Grandpa slammed the gear lever into park and swung open the door in the same motion. He lifted a half-awake Selah from the truck and booted the door closed as she muttered, "Let me sleep."

Dr. Amy was already there watching for them. She looked in Selah's eyes, checked her reflexes, and asked her questions she couldn't answer. She knew her name and her birthday. Otherwise, she said, "I'll have to look it up."

An orderly transferred her to a stretcher and rolled her to X-ray.

Dr. Amy turned to Grandpa. "You were right to get her in here so quick, Ed. I'd say there isn't much doubt she has a concussion."

Grandpa stared at white vinyl tiles on the hospital floor. One hand, thrust deep into the pocket of his faded jeans, rattling his change.

"I've ordered a STAT CT so we'll know more definitively, within the hour. When we know exactly what we're dealing with, we'll talk again. Do you need anything? Some coffee?"

"Just point me to it, doc," he said, his voice quiet and defeated.

"There's a lobby a few doors down. There's always a fresh pot on in there. I'll send the admissions' coordinator to find you, so you can get the formalities done." Dr. Amy walked briskly off to the radiology department to watch over her young patient.

When Selah's parents arrived, they found Grandpa in the ER waiting room with his head buried in his hands. Selah's dad hurried to his dad and wrapped him in a bear-hug. "Where is she?"

"In X-ray."

"I know what you're thinking, Dad. History is not going to repeat itself here." Daniel squeezed Grandpa's shoulder. "Selah always wears a helmet and—"

"It was cracked in half like a walnut."

Dr. Amy bustled into the room. Grandpa and Selah's dad stood. "Amy, you know Selah's parents, Karen and Daniel."

"Yes, from the Hospitality House Fundraiser." She motioned for them to sit. "I've decided to have Selah life-flighted to The Children's Hospital. The CT shows an area of concern, and she began vomiting in X-ray. I think it's best to get her transferred. I've already made the call, and the transport team will be here in less than ten minutes. I consulted with the head of neurology, and he agrees with my assessment. She would be better served in Houston. One parent should fly in with her." Dr. Amy put her arm around Grandpa's shoulder.

Selah's mom stood. "I'll go."

As the news that Selah had slipped into a coma filtered through the close-knit community of Canaan, the people gathered around the family.

Many from Selah's church, plus Grandpa's entire country church, came to The Children's Hospital. Those who couldn't fit in the waiting room overflowed into the hallway. For so many people in the room, it was shockingly quiet.

The pastor bowed his head, and the group prayed in one voice for Selah's healing.

In Selah's room, her mom reached out to rest a hand on her. Her dad nodded his agreement. Selah was pale and deathly still.

Afterward, her dad drifted out of her room to find Grandpa. When he was not in the crowded waiting area, Dad walked to the chapel. Grandpa leaned forward over a chair pulled alongside the pew. Spread out before him were many tattered, treasured pictures of Selah as a three-year-old with his paint horse, Buddy.

"If only I'd looked for my old horse and brought him home for Selah. If she'd been riding Buddy, this wouldn't have happened. That mare..." Grandpa tensed his mouth. "She's a bad seed from bad blood."

On her way to the snack bar, Selah's mom sought out Grandpa. She found him in deep thought in the waiting room and hugged him hard. "It's not your fault, Ed. Selah is a free spirit. She could no more give up riding Dream than stop breathing. She says Dream is her heart-horse."

He sank into a chair with his boots planted a foot apart and his elbows on his knees. His fingers interlaced across his forehead, he shielded his eyes.

Selah's mom sat in the chair beside him and leaned into his shoulder. After a few minutes, she said, "I'm going back to be with Selah. I know Katie is looking after you." She started to walk away then turned back to him. "Ed, I threw some of Selah's jeans in the washer yesterday and found this." She handed him a business card. "A movie producer?"

He took the card and shrugged. "I don't know anything about it."

Grandpa paced around the waiting room. A steady stream of friends drifted through the halls. Katie remained on her knees with several other ladies.

Dr. Steve brought Caroline by the hand. "How's Selah doing?"

Grandpa shook his head. "Not good. Neurologist said 'wait and see'."

Dr. Steve rested his hand on Grandpa's shoulder. "I'm so sorry. Don't worry about the farm. We're looking after it. Dream is doing fine."

"Thank you, doc." Grandpa looked away.

A young lady eased the waiting room door open. "May I come in? I'm Selah's friend from school."

Grandpa's chin popped up. "Of course, you can. You're her new friend. Amanda, right? She would be glad you're here. I'm glad

you're here. It cheers me up to have Selah's friends around. This is Caroline, another friend."

"Hi." Caroline gave a tiny wave. "Selah's told me about you. You got a palomino for Christmas. A dream come true."

Amanda stepped closer to Caroline. "How could this happen to her?"

Caroline shrugged. "I know. She's such a good rider. I'm grateful she was wearing a helmet."

Jordan barged into the room. She made no effort to stifle her tears as she rushed to Grandpa. He hugged her tight and let her cry. When she wiped her eyes, she said, "Cooper's on his way up. The press at the front door thought he might have an update on Selah's condition."

Out the waiting room window overlooking the back parking lot, Grandpa caught a glimpse of pink. He walked to the window, and his mouth dropped open. "Will you look at that?"

Selah's dad peered over Grandpa's shoulder. "Karen should come look. She's with Selah. I'll get her and be right back." He drew Selah's mom into the waiting room and over to the window. Her hand flew to cover her mouth. She closed her eyes, struggling without success to keep the tears back. Pink, crepe paper streamers plastered the huge oak below, and piles upon piles of stuffed ponies mounded the base.

Jordan peeked around Grandpa. "Let's go get Selah some ponies," she said to Caroline and Amanda.

CHAPTER FIFTEEN

A day later, Selah awoke with a shudder. *What a crazy dream.* In the darkened room, a shape was curled up in the chair. "Miss Katie?"

Katie woke instantly and sprang to the bedside. "Selah. Oh, Selah. Thank God. Your grandpa's in the chapel. I'll get him right away." She pushed the nurse call button and yelled into the plastic grate on the wall. "Send a nurse, send a nurse. Selah is awake!" As the nurse rushed in, Katie rushed out. "Notify Dr. Amy, immediately. I'm going to get Selah's family."

Calling Grandpa's name, Katie ran down the hospital hallway. She flew into the chapel and crashed headlong into him. "Ed! Selah is awake! Hurry."

Their friends from church erupted in joyful celebration.

Katie didn't bother to wipe the tears gushing from her eyes. "Where are her parents?"

"In the cafeteria."

"You go to her. I'll get them."

Grandpa hugged Katie tight. "Thank God."

She ran into the cafeteria and scanned the room for Selah's parents. She hurried around the crowded area and called above the noise. "Karen, Daniel, are you here?"

Selah's mom leapt to her feet, spilling sweet tea all over the table. "Over here!"

"Excuse me." Katie squeezed through. "Excuse me." She nearly crushed the breath out of Selah's mom. "She's awake."

Selah's parents grasped hands over the corner of the table as their eyes met. They hurried after Katie.

Selah lay propped up by mountains of pillows in the hospital bed, surrounded by stuffed ponies, crunching ice chips. She smiled as her family came rumbling in and gathered her in a collective hug.

"I'm so grateful to have you back." Mom clung to her. "Could you hear us?" Mom finally asked. "Could you hear us talking to you and praying for you?"

"No, I don't think so. It felt like I was somewhere else. Like I crossed a time warp, went to another dimension or something." Selah's voice got shrill. "I don't understand what happened."

"Calm down, sweetie. You're with us and safe." Mom slid stuffed pink ponies aside and sat beside Selah.

"I'm so confused."

Mom searched Selah's eyes. "You fell off Dream and hit your head."

"All I remember was a bright light and a super loud boom."

"Sounds like lightning," Grandpa said. "There were small storms in the area. I didn't think they were serious."

Dr. Amy knocked on the door as she pushed it open. "I hear there's a party going on!"

Grandpa slapped his hand on his thigh and put his thumb up. "We got our miracle, Amy."

"Glad to have you back with us." Dr. Amy examined Selah and entered notes into the computer system. "My prescription for you is to keep things quiet for a couple weeks. And I know your first question, and the answer is—no riding."

"Yes, ma'am." Selah turned to Grandpa. "Did I miss the benefit for Mr. Classan's ranch?"

Grandpa shook his head. "You didn't miss it, but you're not riding either."

Dr. Amy never looked up from her clipboard. "I would err on the side of caution. I'm not giving the green light for anything strenuous until some time has passed. We'll do more testing tomorrow and plan your discharge based on those results."

The next day after all her tests, Selah slept the afternoon away. As she woke, she felt someone staring at her. "You wouldn't think I would need so much sleep since all I've done is lay in this bed."

Katie moved to her side to arrange the pillows. "Sleep is for healing."

"Where is everyone?"

"Your grandpa went to get coffee. He either got lost or ran into someone he knows—again. Your dad is outside talking to a man in a uniform who came to see you. Your mom went home to get your brothers."

"It must be Deputy Bob. He loves me. Did you use essential oils on me like you did for Buddy?"

Katie grinned. "Frankincense and myrrh."

"I figured. Do you have an oil for everything?"

"Pretty much."

"Thank you for being here, Miss Katie. For me and for Grandpa. I don't know how moving is going to work out, but deep in my heart, I know it's not your fault I can't live at the farm." Selah lowered her eyes and twisted the bedsheet in her hands. "Lately, I've been feeling like an evil alien lives in my head. I'm sorry for how awful I've been to you."

"Thirteen can be a rough year, but we'll get through it," Katie promised with a kindness Selah knew she didn't deserve. "Your apology is accepted."

Grandpa slipped into the room and tossed Selah a paperback book with a blood bay foal on the cover. "Look what I found in the gift shop."

She clutched the book to her chest and grinned at him. "A horse book I haven't read. Thank you."

Then he handed her a large workbook and a sketchpad. "Your grandma would have taught you to draw." He smiled over at Katie.

Selah followed his gaze and wondered why she hadn't considered it already. "Oh, would you teach me, Miss Katie?" she whispered, already envisioning her walls covered in drawings of Sweet Dream.

Before Katie could answer, Selah's dad opened the door wide. "Guess who's hanging out in the hall?" He ushered in a vaguely familiar face. "A visitor for you. I'm going to get some coffee. Can I get anything for you, folks?"

The slightly familiar man, Grandpa, and Katie all gave a quick shake of their heads.

Selah asked the uniformed man, "Do I know you?"

"We were never properly introduced, were we? I'm Mark." The forest ranger stepped forward and offered his hand. "I don't want to intrude, but I was never able to thank you properly. I have three little boys that need me, and I'm grateful beyond words I get to tell you now. I owe my life to you. Thank you."

A flicker of recognition crossed her mind. "You're the ranger in the plane. I remember. I only did the right thing."

"You're one brave girl, and I want to meet that horse of yours someday."

"I was scared to death. That doesn't feel brave."

"Of course, you were. What you did was dangerous, but you did it anyway." Mark smiled at her. "You need your rest, young lady. Get well."

"It was nice of you to come," Katie interjected. "Thank you."

"I'd love to hear the story of how you brought that horse from wild to being able to pull me out of a plane, but I can't stay." He fumbled with his cap. "When my project manager quit without notice, he put me in a bind." As he turned for the door, he waved his cap at her. "I need to get back to the office, but when I heard you were here, I wanted to stop by and express my appreciation. I'm glad I got to tell you thank you."

"Wait. Please wait."

He turned back.

"What does a project manager do?"

"They are second in command of the branch office. They have to handle everything from the operational budget to scheduling the volunteers. Are you applying for a job?" He chuckled.

"Do they need good computer skills?"

"Those are critical." He reached for the door handle.

"I know someone who would be perfect."

His grin told her, he thought she was joking. "Oh, thanks, Selah, but there is a bureaucratic system to screen applicants."

"But if the person was really, really perfect for the job, wouldn't you want them?"

The ranger chuckled again and shook his head. "I've gotta go."

"But my dad—"

Balancing his coffee and a donut on a napkin, Selah's dad pushed open the door.

"My dad would be perfect, and he needs a job." When everyone just stared at her, she added, "And we won't have to move to California!"

The two men gawked at each other speechless.

"My dad can do anything." Selah smiled hopefully and stutter nodded. "And he's a hard worker."

The ranger looked at the faces around the room before his gaze rested on Selah. "Um..." he stammered. After another minute of awkward silence, the ranger asked Dad, "Can we talk in the hall?"

Her dad set his coffee and donut down and followed Mark outside.

Grandpa stood and stretched. "You are something else. If I hadn't heard that myself, I wouldn't have believed it."

"Now, Ed." Katie put her hand on his arm. "Girls are raised these days to speak their mind."

Selah grinned.

When her dad finally came back, he wore a dazed expression. "You are a trip." He kissed Selah on the forehead. "If you ever pull a stunt like that again, you won't come out of your room for two weeks."

"Oh. Guess it didn't go very good. Sorry." She grimaced. "I tried to help."

"I thought nothing could embarrass me at this point in my life. You proved me wrong. I was mortified at your antics."

She averted her eyes and twisted the sheet into a wad.

"Did you think you could just bend the rules of the Forest Service to your will?"

Something in his tone made Selah snap her head up. She caught the faint twinkle in his eye. She scrunched her brows together. "What happened?"

"He's quite a nice man, actually. I have to go fill out all the application forms tomorrow and pass a background check, but I have a job."

She pitched a stuffed horse at her dad, and he lobbed it back at her. Glee surged through her heart and bubbled from her mouth. "You'll be great at it! We don't have to move!"

Dad's face crumpled and told her a sad story. "Actually, we will still be moving."

"Oh." She slumped as the disappointment registered.

"While you were in the hospital, we got a great contract offer on our house. We weren't thinking too clearly because of the situation with you, but we thought we were unlikely to get another offer so good. They wanted their daughter in the elementary nearby, and we needed to move to California so we accepted it."

She swallowed hard. "You sold our house. I so hoped we wouldn't have to move."

The door eased open, and Vanessa peeked in. "Is it okay to come in?"

Katie beckoned her. "Of course. Welcome."

"I can't stay long. My father is waiting in the car. If you hear honking—that's him." As Vanessa extended a book, Selah slid the covers over the one on her bed. "Wow. A horse book I haven't read.

Thank you." She flipped the book over to read the description on the back. "Have you read it? Is it good?"

"Oh yeah. It's the story of best friends. One is in a wheelchair, but she loves horses. The other girl has horses and fixes up a saddle so they can ride together. They get in so much trouble." Vanessa smiled big. "You will—love—it."

"Thank you. It was very, very nice of you to come see me. I can't wait to read the book."

Vanessa's gaze dropped to the floor. "I wanted to say sorry about the things I posted on Facelook."

Vanessa's chin snapped up, and their eyes met.

Selah nodded forgiveness.

Vanessa gave a little wave but a bigger smile as she slipped away.

Selah's eyebrows shot up as she noticed a conspiracy huddle in the corner. "Grandpa. What are you whispering about over there?"

He beamed a smile at her. "We are grateful our flower girl is awake." He put his arm around Katie, and they moved to the foot of the bed. "I like my plan to sell our farms and travel the world together. I want to go to Israel and Italy and Iceland and Ireland."

Katie nudged him with her elbow. "She gets the idea."

Suspicion twisted Selah's lips to a confused frown. "Why are you smiling at me when you're telling me you can't wait to leave?"

He chuckled. "Because you're due a little torment after what you put us through."

Katie chimed in, "It would never have worked because, just like you could never give up Dream, I can't give up my farm—my lambs."

"We've decided to live at her place after the wedding," added Grandpa.

Selah jolted upright in the hospital bed. "We can buy your farm! And I can take care of Katie's sheep while you travel. I didn't know it, but I love lambs. It's what I've always hoped for. Can we, Dad? Can we?" She reached for his arm.

"Make way for the Selah express." He mashed his face with his hands as he slid them down his face. "I'll have to talk to your mom, but considering the job is in the Canaan office it only makes sense."

"I'm...*moving*...to the farm?" She looked from one face to another in disbelief. "I'll be with Dream—*every* day? Wait, this isn't a crazy dream, is it? Would somebody pinch me?"

"Not a dream, honey." Katie leaned over to look into Selah's eyes. "And something that would make me very happy—I hope you'll call me Grandma Katie now? I love you like you're my own."

Selah started to cry when she saw tears in Katie's eyes. "I love you, too, Grandma Katie."

"There could be no better wedding present." Grandpa blew his nose. After a few moments, he said, "Come on, Katie." He sniffled. "Time for us to go. We've a wedding to plan. Love you, sunshine. Rest." He kissed the top of Selah's head.

"Katie." Selah called after her, then whispered, "Does Grandpa know about our special guest?"

Katie's mouth formed a soundless no.

"What's that about?" Dad asked as they left.

Her eyes twinkled. "A little secret Katie and I share."

CHAPTER SIXTEEN

*F*our weeks later, the announcer nearly shouted, "Selah! And Sweet Dream!" Thunderous applause rocked the stadium while the colored spotlights twirled over the arena, the audience, and the ceiling. The light finally focused on a diminutive girl dressed completely in pink and her black mare. Selah ran like a dancer into the arena waving at the crowd, and Dream trotted with energy beside her. Her nose right at Selah's elbow. Nothing bound them together except love.

The plan had been for Selah to wave and bow. Perhaps make a small circle and leave. But the applause quickened. In the center of the arena, Selah asked Dream to kneel, hesitated a moment, but then slid onto her back. Stroking her neck and mane, Selah cued the mare for a canter much to the horror of her grandfather.

After a couple minutes, Cooper's media director adjusted the sound booth controls and started the melody Selah loved. And the beautiful pair danced. A hush fell over the stadium, and every eye soaked in Selah's celebration of an obvious, complete recovery. The crowd expressed adoration for Selah and Dream with soft oohs and ahhs.

Kneeling in the arena dust, Mr. Classan kept his lens trained on the pair. So great was the joy in Selah's heart, the photographs reflected her love and passion for riding.

Selah's friends, Vanessa, Amanda, and Caroline beamed smiles. Next to Amanda was Cindy, the owner of the barn where Amanda boarded her golden pony. Clutching her hands beneath her chin, Cindy stared at the dancing pair. She leaned heavily onto the shoulder of her husband, who produced the greatest horse movie ever made. With rapt attention, he considered the infinite possibilities.

Their souls stirred by sweet perfection, Cindy took her husband by the hand, and they made their way directly to the arena exit intent on intercepting the Sweet Dream duo. As Cindy introduced herself and her husband, Selah danced with joy from one pink booted foot to the other. Dream also danced at the end of her lead line absorbing the energy Selah broadcasted. Life was about to change forever, even beyond her wildest dreams. Her face reflected the wonder of it all.

CHAPTER SEVENTEEN

Perfect day for an outdoor wedding. Wait till you see the surprise we have for you, Grandpa. Selah peeked through the bushes at Grandpa already standing by the altar set up near Katie's rose garden. *He looks happy enough to bust his buttons off his fancy vest.*

At Grandpa's elbow, Mr. Cooper adjusted his suit coat then his tie. He shifted, appearing uncomfortable without his work jeans and boots. Both her little brothers, dressed in little suits and ties, hovered near Grandpa. Michael squirmed and tugged at his tucked shirt. As Davy fidgeted with his tie, he kept his eyes fixed on Grandpa. Mr. Classan stood off to the side with his camera poised.

His hands clasped behind him, Grandpa waited. When Selah appeared under the arch, their eyes met. His face lit up, and he smiled as big as Texas. Her dress was a sassy shade of pink with a white sash. Her new pink boots, a thank-you gift from Katie, sparkled with bling. She held a bouquet of white flowers, and a wide ribbon wafted behind her. As she stepped forward, an old, beloved, paint horse followed her through the arch. Long white ribbons laced through Buddy's mane, and flowers studded his white halter. Across his withers hung a shawl of white and purple flowers and greenery with a few sprigs nibbled short.

At the shocked look on Grandpa's face, happy tears flowed down Selah's cheeks. She'd waited a long time for this moment. Chuckles came from the small group of friends gathered, and Selah followed their gaze to peek back at Buddy. He lipped and vacuumed up a few flower petals as he trailed her down the aisle.

When they arrived at the altar, Selah offered Buddy's ribbon lead to Grandpa. Grandpa grabbed his old friend by the halter and planted a big kiss on his muzzle. He rubbed the sides of Buddy's face and neck. "I can't believe it. Wow! I can't wait to hear the story behind this."

Selah moved Buddy to his place of honor beside Davy and Michael.

When the wedding march began, everyone rose and turned toward the arch to look for Miss Katie. *Grandma Katie now.* She floated through the arch flanked with tall flowering shrubs. Moving with dignified grace in dainty steps, she reigned like royalty in her layered satin gown embellished with swirls of white pearls. Selah's dad eased to Katie's side. She took his arm, and he walked her down the flower-strewn aisle to Grandpa.

Selah couldn't take her eyes off Grandpa's face as he watched Katie come toward him. He took Katie's hand in his, patted it, and they turned to the altar.

The minister preached about family, love, and marriage. When he called for the ring, Michael and Davy led Buddy forward. Grandpa untied the ribbon on his forelock securing the wedding rings. He chuckled and smiled at Selah. "Be happy for me," he whispered to her.

Her eyes blurred, and Selah could hardly speak. "I love you. You're the best grandpa ever."

Dear Reader:

If you enjoyed this book, please take a minute to help other people find it by sharing a review.

Sign up on my website for new release notification so you will find out about the next book as soon as it is available. Also, for any contests or giveaways—join me at http://www.susancount.com/

Hearing from readers encourages me to keep writing. E-mail a comment: susancountauthor@yahoo.com

Please like Susan Count at http://www.facebook.com/susancount where I post only horse related videos.

I'm also on Twitter: https://twitter.com/SusanCount
And Pinterest: https://www.pinterest.com/susancount/

Award Winning
DREAM HORSE ADVENTURES
Series

MARY'S SONG–BOOK 1
A girl and a foal share one thing. They are both
lame. One cannot survive without the other.

SELAH'S SWEET DREAM–BOOK 2
A girl with a dream to be an equestrian
superstar. A horse with ATTITUDE.

SELAH'S PAINTED DREAM–BOOK 3
One word can ruin a perfect life—moving.

SELAH'S STOLEN DREAM–BOOK 4
One girl's victory is the other's tragic defeat.

READER REVIEWS:
Best horse books ever. Charming. Action packed.
Heart-warming. Page turner. I'm utterly smitten.
Stole my heart. Good for the soul.

ABOUT WRITING...

How many twists and turns can one person take before they figure out what they were born to do? My degree is in Applied Science – nothing in that prepared me to write novels for children. But the writing process gave me great joy and restored my spirit after a season of loss.

The passion behind my work is renewed from letters that come from young fans. One recently told me she felt like she was riding in the buggy with Mary and Laura in *Mary's Song*. A grandmother admonished me to stop saying the books are juvenile fiction because she adored them and it made her feel like she was twelve-years-old again. Love from fans keeps me writing.

I adore grandchildren, horses, bunnies, mochas, the beach, forest trails, and especially joy found in the Lord. Instilled with the need to create, I love building projects and writing adventure stories. I am a life-long equestrian and am owned by a Rocky Mountain Horse. Though I am a rider and lover of horses, I make no claims of expertise in any riding discipline and each book requires thorough research to avoid annoying those who would know.

I write at an antique secretary desk that occupies a glass room with a forest view. Fittingly, it once belonged to the same wise grandmother who introduced me to the love of reading via Walter Farley's horse books. That desk has *secret* compartments which hold memories, mysteries, and story ideas.

The only thing more fun than riding might be writing horse adventure stories and I invite you to saddle up and ride along.

Made in the USA
Columbia, SC
17 July 2020

14126037R00111